Mama Rock's Rules

{ Ten Lessons for Raising a Houseful of Successful Children }

Rose Rock

with Valerie Graham

COLLINS LIVING
An Imprint of HarperCollins Publishers

HarperCollins books may be purchased for educational, business, or sales promotional use. For information, please write: Special Markets Department, HarperCollins Publishers, 10 East 53rd Street, New York, NY 10022.

First Collins Living paperback edition published 2009.

Designed by Richard Oriolo

Library of Congress Cataloging-in-Publication Data is available upon request.

ISBN 978-0-06-153612-0
ISBN 978-0-06-153611-3 (pbk.)

14 ♦/RRD   10   9   8   7   6   5

To all the strong Mamas of the village, circa "The Hill,"
Andrews, South Carolina

Contents

Foreword

I FIRST MET ROSE ROCK ON February 7, 1965, the day I was allegedly born. She rescued me from a man in a white lab jacket who had just smacked me on the butt. She claimed to be my mother and I had no identification or cash on me at the time, so when she offered to take me home I didn't put up much of a fuss.

In the years to follow, Rose and Julius (my father) raised me, my five brothers, and one sister without any of us dropping dead. Now that might not sound like much, but where I'm from, Bedford-Stuyvesant, Brooklyn, where four out of five black men are either dead, in jail, or making a rap CD, it's a major accomplishment.

As of the writing of this foreword, none of Rose's children has a criminal record or has had any baby mommas. How did Rose and my father pull off this miracle? With a little love, a lot of understanding, and a good belt.

—Chris Rock

Prologue

THIS BOOK ACTUALLY BEGAN MORE than forty-two years ago. Of course, I want to believe it was all my idea, but actually, my parents, Pearl and Wesley Tingman, had already laid the foundation. I was so blessed to have them as my parents—even though it took me many years to see that. They taught me that children deserved security, respect, and most of all, love. They taught me to place value on my actions and myself. They often said that a good name was worth more than wealth. I passed those values on to my children: the children of Rose and Julius Rock were expected to behave in a certain manner.

To be a parent is and should be a calling. There is absolutely nothing as great, challenging, or rewarding as raising a child. In writing this book I hope to show parents that their role deserves reverence and respect.

The ten most important rules I live by are covered in this book. Each chapter focuses on an important concept and how to bring it home for you. In every section you will find stories and examples from my family and some comments from each of my children—along with some specific strategies to help you along. My best secret weapons are in the Mama's Mojo sections.

Rules make life easier, because they spell out exactly what to do for a given situation. My Mama Rock's rules are designed for parents to help their children grow into responsible, strong, loving, independent adults, and to pass it on, so when they have their own children, they will teach the same strong values and morals.

Hopefully, as you read about my rules and strategies, you will find things you can relate to that fit into your own idea of child rearing. One thing for sure—rules make things easier for both parent and child. However, any rule can be modified to fit into your own individual situation. And, in all things, remember the main truth: *You are the parent!*

I am still singing my parents' songs and the songs of the people whose shoulders I stood on. I hope my children will be a full-blown orchestra singing the songs of Julius and me, their grandparents, and all those who have gone before them.

Who's Who and What's What: An Introduction to Mama Rock's Family

ALL THE KIDS ON THE block wanted to hang out in our big, brownstone house in Brooklyn, New York, at 619 Decatur Street. We lived there for almost twenty-five years. Sometimes our children, friends, and family would fill up the whole place. My husband Julius and I were also second parents to some special young people.

Here's the actual cast of characters who grew up in our family: Julius's son, my stepson, Charles, "Shabazz"—who passed away three years ago—was a full-time member of our family and an

Chris

Andre

619 Decatur Street

Tony

Brian

Kenny

Andi

Jordan

idol to his younger brothers; Chris—"Chrissy"—a comedian, director, and father of my two granddaughters, Lola and Zarah; Andre, owner of Julius Rock Trucking Company and father to my three grandsons, Caleb, Judah, and Thawada; Tony—"Tone"—a comedian and an actor on UPN's *All of Us* TV show; Brian, a minister and corporate specialist; Kenny, self-employed and a rising actor; Andrea—"Andi"—a Winthrop University student in broadcast journalism; and Jordan, a high school student and comic.

Mary Allison Williams and Elizabeth Ann Pitcher were not birth children but they are our children—the children of our hearts. Mary Allison—"Ally"—is now Dr. Mary Williams, a professor at Grove City College in Pennsylvania. Elizabeth is a social worker with the school system in St. David's Island, Bermuda.

We were also second parents to Randy Richardson, Chris's best friend, who was so close to us Julius bought an extra bed for him in our house. Randy is now the second in command for the New York City subway system. Then there is Mervin "Spectac" Jenkins, whom I call "my son." He is a middle school principal and a rap artist.

If you start back in 1969, you can count more than seventeen foster children who shared our home. And that's saying nothing about the scores of other children who will always feel like part of our great, big extended family.

Mama Rock's Rules

{ 1 }

I Am Your Mama,
Not Your Friend

I NEVER FELT THE NEED TO be friends with my children—not
when they were eight or ten. Not even when they were sixteen
years old. My kids had their own friends and I had mine. I
never set out to win any popularity contests on the home front.
Like my mother, I know my kids don't have to like me—neither
do yours.

My mother's overall message was a good one; I finally understand it: being a parent is not about being right, it's about *doing*
right. It's about serving as a steadfast role model for your children,

no matter what. Children really do look to adults for examples and guidance (you just never meet a teenager who would admit it).

Here's a secret: I didn't even like my mother until I was forty years old. Did I love her? Yes. I also respected her. Sure, when I was growing up I resented her when she was right about things—and, believe me, she always was.

Andre: I thought my mother didn't know what she was talking about. But, let me tell you, I found out she knew everything. I didn't give her enough credit, especially when she told me about women. However, she was right. Now, I tell my kids they've got to listen to their Mama (my wife).

Be honest. When you first had your baby were you torn between being a parent and a friend to the child? In my world, there is no decision to make. It was made when you had your child. As a parent, you are responsible for your child's mental, emotional, and spiritual growth. Your friends don't ask you to be accountable for them in the same way, do they?

After all, I don't tell my friends what to do or punish them if they don't keep a promise to me (OK, I usually act kind of cool toward them for awhile, but you know what I mean). I don't make rules for them and certainly never enforce any. My friends also don't expect me to provide their security or be their protector.

You ask me: Mama Rock, can't I be both a parent and a friend to my children? Listen, when parents say they want to be friends with a child it is usually about pleasing the child; after all, no one likes friction. Every parent must have the courage to be in charge and to say no. You can have fun with your kids just like you can with a friend—we had plenty of fun—but you can't be afraid to enforce the rules because you might lose your child's affection. As parents, we have to protect our children. That is a job for a parent—not a friend.

Draw the Line to Win Respect

Just as I talk differently to my children than I would to my friends, I expect my children to talk differently to me than they would to their friends. Once, when Andi was a teenager, we were together in the car having a funny, *girl* conversation about boys. I don't remember what I said, but suddenly she blurted out, "You lie, that's just a lie!" I felt like throwing her out of the car. Then I realized I had allowed that moment. I had to quietly remind her I was not her girlfriend; there were certain things she was not allowed to say to me, ever.

I think there are topics (like *girl* talk) where you can be friendly or joke around

Brian: My father didn't try to be our friend and neither did my mother. They were our parents. Friends were people who liked you and who you liked; mutual feelings and all that. It damages a child when you only act like a friend. They will think the world revolves around them and always will.

without having to be a stern parent. But, at no time should you let your children think they can disrespect you or treat you like a buddy. It's never OK for your child to disrespect you in any way, at any time, for any reason. They need to know that up front. We've all seen those crazy mothers on *Maury* or *Jerry Springer.* You know, the ones who complain how their children—even ten-year-olds—talk back to them. I want to shout to the TV screen: *"Hey lady, you are the parent, you need to draw the line and get some respect for yourself."*

The message to children is this: you cannot live in my house, spend my money, and disrespect me. It is that simple. I don't hand out freebies. Brian remembers one time when he was angry with me for not allowing him to go somewhere with a friend. He started to yell at me. I said to him: "*Where is YOUR child you are yelling at? I don't see any child, I just see your Mama being yelled at, and you are in some big trouble.*"

Start Early to Stay Strong

So how to start being a good, strong parent? First and foremost, establish a hierarchy about who is in charge in your family. It's really quite simple:

Rule #1: I am the Parent. I make the rules.
Rule #2: You are the child. You follow the rules.
Rule #3: Any problems, refer to Rule #1.

The whole thing with rules is this: it's all about responsibility. When you make guidelines, it makes life easier, it manages expectations. Don't wait! Start early and start them young.

What happens if you don't? Well, have you ever seen parents who allow a toddler to hit them in the face because they think it's so cute? Later, when the child is five or six and hits them in front of others, they are embarrassed. What if the kid keeps on punching when he or she is older? Think about that. Negative behavior like that means the parents started the rules too late (or not at all). Listen up: if you don't stop those things early, you will be scared of your own child in your own house.

Think about it this way: approach child rearing like you would if you had a flat tire on your car. As soon as you feel the first jolt of the flat, you stop and change it, right? If you try and drive to the nearest station (even if it's only a few blocks away) the tire will be damaged and the rim will be bent out of shape. The same holds true when you raise a child. Stop and regroup at the first blowout. Provide a powerful, initial action or consequence when the offensive behavior first occurs so you won't end up bent out of shape.

So, when your baby tries to hit mommy or daddy, touch something dangerous, or do something inappropriate—move fast. Redirect your child right away to something else—anything else—a toy, a book, even a funny sound. Do it every time to refocus their attention. This is important, as it is more effective to redirect a child's attention from the wrong behavior than to snatch the offending thing away or grab their hands too hard. That only sets off a kid's crying jag—it does nothing for learning. Sometimes, kids start to wail because they know it will get your interest when they do it. Yes, they are that smart.

I've seen people slap a little kid's hand when they try to hit or touch the wrong thing. Come on, that is good for nothin' because it doesn't teach the right behavior. Worse, sometimes the same parent turns around and spanks the kid for crying because his hand hurts. That reaction is just about the dumbest thing I have ever seen.

Don't Hide the Cookie Jar

As I said earlier, children are never too young for rules. They can better appreciate the rules if parents allow them to understand how behavior becomes a matter of choice. Your child, even as a little one, can learn to avoid bad consequences and seek good reinforcements through their actions.

In setting up your rules, it is important to balance a child's need for exploration and freedom with safety. Start at square one with a few practical plans. For instance, early in your parenting career you should baby-proof your house to some extent so you do not constantly have to say no every time your baby turns around. But, you don't need to go overboard and remove everything. If you do, it will be hard to take your child to someone else's un-baby-proofed house. Do the basics, of course, and remove obviously harmful items. After you take care of that, make it possible—by your rules—to allow your child to move around in the house and make the right choices.

The Cookie Contracts

It's all about balance. Don't make something completely forbidden. After all, if children think a thing is forbidden, it will become even more enticing. For example, I think it's plain horrible to have treats in your house and have to keep them hidden. Of course, I am not referring to Mama's valentine chocolates. No one gets those except Mama. I am talking about things your children use—like the cookie jar; they should be kept at a kid-appropriate level so they can get at them when the time is right. This is where the Cookie Contract comes in.

Chris started out as the oldest in our cookie world. He knew how many cookies he could have and when he could have them because I set the cookie boundaries—it was an informal "cookie contract." Because our cookie jar was not *forbidden*, it was no big deal. All the other boys followed suit. When we said to go ahead and have a few cookies, that's exactly what they did (even the youngest ones). No one had to sneak.

Don't Forget the Hug Factor

Remember this: every consequence your child experiences because he did not follow a rule should be something he can learn from and apply to his future behavior. Parenting should never be only about punishment—or you need help way beyond the scope of this book.

Be sure to offer some reward just for being good—that's a top incentive. It makes a child's choice clearer if hugs and kisses are given for good behavior, at least sometimes. Let your child know the specific good behavior that earned a big dose of positive attention. If you do that, kids won't be tempted to do so many "bad" things to get that attention.

Keep in mind what is age appropriate as you begin. For example, the smallest child can learn to say "please" and "thank you." Add on new rules or expand them as your children mature. Here's another way of getting your kids to understand boundaries: assign your child a toy chest and a clothes hamper. You can start as early as two years old. (Don't sit there and tell me you can't do this because you don't have a big toy chest or a fancy hamper.) Go to the nearest value store and get each child a basket and hamper—those stores have laundry baskets and those pop-open hampers for a buck. The laundry baskets are helpful for toys. If you have more than one child, give each a different color. Here's how it worked for me: I'd announce it was clean-up time for all toys right before dinner. The consequences of not doing so were that the toys would "disappear" for a week.

Now, on to the laundry: tell the kids to take off their dirty socks at a certain time and put them in their own hamper where they belong. If you have a few kids, make it into a contest: who can get the dirty clothes in their hamper the fastest? If it's your first child, make a big deal with your watch or count out loud. Kids really like games and a sense of order in the chaos.

> **MAMA'S MOJO** If your child is too little, have a laundry basket available for him where he can easily reach it—right in his room. All he'll have to do is toddle in and pop those dirty clothes into the basket. It's easy for him and you've started the trend.

When you are busy ironing or sorting laundry, nothing works better than a big laundry basket of socks (could be your unmatched pairs) for something to keep your child busy. Kids can take the socks in and out of the basket and have a great time. Ally has a vivid memory of when she would play in the sock basket while I was ironing. I must have been happy too, because she remembers hearing me sing during those times. I probably was singing because I didn't have to scold a little girl who happily played in the sock basket.

Join the Congregation of Expectations

Setting your rule expectations is the most important thing you can do for your children. You must state clearly what you want. Then, remind them again—at least once. The main expectation to convey is simple: you require your child to listen and follow you.

> **MAMA'S MOJO** Look your children square in the eye when you make rules and requests. This is no time to be wishy-washy. Speak strongly (don't scream). Ask them to repeat what you said so there's no problem later on with what went down. Listen up: if your kids *always* agree with everything you say, you've got another problem—either they don't care what you say, or you are not asking enough from them.

Long before you and your child ever get in a car or set foot in a grocery store, restaurant, or friend's house, you need to talk about what kind of behavior is expected. Create realistic expectations of what will happen when you are at these places. Believe me, they have no idea—especially when they are young. You need to spell it out exactly.

For example, an important grocery store rule is: *look with your eyes and not with your hands.* Before we entered a store, I would outline the action plan. For example, I'd tell the kids we can get two cereals today—one sweet and one regular. Then, I'd assign one child to pick out the sweet cereal and another to pick the regular. Maybe I'd tell a younger one to choose a favorite snack for us to take home. If everyone behaved well in the store, that snack was to be the reward.

If we were going somewhere like Wal-Mart, I might say, "We are not buying today." That way, the kids knew before we went into stores that toys and such would not be purchased. Don't wait until you are in the store to announce this—if you do, you end up having to say no, repeatedly. Reinforce what you came to buy in the first place.

One time, when I was at a store, I happened to overhear a mother tell her young son, "If you behave, I'll buy you a nice toy." The boy promptly sat up straight in the cart, full of expectation. Our carts would pass as we browsed the aisles—each time the little boy was happy and quiet. Then, on her way over to the housewares section, the mother passed by a big toy display. Of course, her son was all excited because the promised toys were in sight. Instead of picking one out and putting it in the basket, the mother pushed the cart away from the toys and kept on walking. The boy started to cry. The mother became angry and things escalated fast. Later, I saw the mother go out of the store with her weepy child (and no toys). Honor the expectations you create. It is a mistake not to do it; what do you think will happen the next time these two go to a store?

> **MAMA'S MOJO** Here's some *great toy mojo*: If we'd go shopping anywhere with lots of toys, I'd put a few of the sturdy ones in the basket with my boys. They'd be busy with the toy and play with it (I only used nonbreakables). Usually, by the time we got to checkout, they didn't even care about that toy. Then, we'd either leave or I'd get them something small and they would be happy.

Rules for visiting a friend's house begin with a reminder to *be on your best behavior.* These rules should include reminding your child to use his quieter "inside voice," not his noisier "outside voice." Kids have to be reminded about their noise level because they laugh often and express emotions out loud—much more than we adults do. That's great, but not inside the four walls at someone's home, or sometimes inside your own house.

Once, during a visit to a friend's house, a place where everyone always had a good time, there was a young girl with manners that were not just good, they were great. I had to compliment her. She told me her mother said the trick to a return invitation was to have good manners. What a smart idea to keep kids on the right behavior track at a place they enjoy and want to see again.

The Truth About Consequences

Parents, you have to be tough enough. Get up your nerve to leave the grocery store in the middle of shopping or doggy bag your restaurant meal and go home. You have to do it. Otherwise, you'll feel like you have déjà vu everywhere you go—Oh no, he's doing it again! Sure, it will mean the hassle of going back to the store or wherever, but think of the time and energy you'll have to sacrifice if you have to deal with awful behavior as the norm rather than the exception.

But also remember to be realistic. Children who are tired, hungry, or both cannot be expected to exhibit their best behavior. Many times, parents have to compromise their schedules in the best interest of their children. After all, when you have no kids you can pick up and do what you want. For example, maybe you like to go grocery shopping at 10 P.M. when everything is less crowded. That's fine, but don't expect your little child to handle it well. We've all seen a parent who tries to shop with her kid long past any child's decent bedtime. The child is often exhausted, so he ends up crying or whining. Then—guess what—the parent yells or slaps him to keep quiet and he cries again. Unless it is urgent, plan for a better time to do your necessary activities (or, see if you can get someone to watch your child).

Remember, any explanation of rules must be followed by specifics about what happens if rules are not followed. This can be anything from a time-out (public or private) to loss of certain privileges like TV or outings. Be flexible. If your kid broke the rules at Grandma's house, it makes no sense to say you are not going back there ever again—you know you can't avoid Grandma. So, enact the "no TV" penalty phase instead. Otherwise, you will look like a fool.

Get in Touch with Your Big Bad Wolf

Yeah, if you are the parent, you have to be the one responsible for everything—and you have to be the enforcer. Sometimes, you do have to be unpopular like the *Big Bad Wolf*. You can't be pals with your kids and then turn around and enforce punishment—that shape-shifting doesn't work. You need to be consistent.

It's best to stand tough with your house rules. Then you don't need to be a policeman or a big, bad *you-know-what*. With all the outside influences children deal with today, strong parents are needed more than ever. If you don't impart a sense of respect and of boundaries, you are not parenting. And, if you think your kids will be prepared for the "real world" with all of its everyday frustrations, you've got another thing coming.

Remember, what you don't teach them the world will—and it won't be kind about it. The government, police, and others will deal with your children if they go astray. Once in that system, everyone loses.

If you do not establish boundaries for your children, you deny them the skills they need to cope with life's problems. Even if they don't have any problems now (because you shielded them from every consequence or disappointment), they will probably have big troubles down the road, because life is not a bowl of cherries. Maybe that's the real history behind the latest rush of stars and sports figures in jail or in rehab.

Warnings May Be Bad for Your Health

Warnings are fine on a pack of cigarettes. I don't like warnings used as threats for misbehavior, as in *don't come in late again or you'll be grounded for a week*. If the formula is set (a certain broken rule = a particular consequence), ditch the warnings. Threats with no follow-through are no good. At least, act on the second threat if you can't stop yourself from another warning. If you are all talk and no action as a parent, you are a bad disciplinarian.

Andre: I notice that if my wife says something over and over, my kids know by the second time she's not going to do anything. They got her number, they stopped listening because they figured she was all talk. But, it's never too late to change.

If I call upstairs, my child better come down. If I have to call a second time and go up there, he'd better be sleeping or unconscious. Don't say something unless you mean it. My kids knew we meant it!

The Scoop on the Snoop

Some parents tell me their kids inform them their bedrooms are off limits. Are you kidding me? In what world do these parents live? Newsflash: everything in the whole house belongs to the parents. This includes the kid's room and everything in it.

Being ordered to stay away from your child's room by that child is not acceptable. Being ordered to do anything by your child is not acceptable. As a parent, you need to be a winner in the authority game. You do this by having a clear line about who is in charge—namely, you. If you've lost your authority, take it back. It's better if you didn't lose it in the first place—by acting like a friend—but it's not too late to grab it back. Do it now.

On the other hand, unless you suspect problems with illegal or dangerous activities, there is no good reason to snoop around your child's room. Andi had all kinds of notes strewn around her room when she was a teenager. Once, I picked one up and started to read it. I discovered it was only about her personal stuff and gossip. She trusted me enough to leave those notes out in the open, so I needed to trust her enough not to go back and read them all—even if I wanted to.

Now, if I thought she was on drugs or something else I'd pull out the mattress and rip through her closet. Some parents do that kind of thing anyway, just to be all up in their kid's business. There is no need for that; certain privacies must be observed—children do deserve a certain respect.

Don't Just Set the Table: Set a Good Example

You simply must set a good example. Who hasn't heard "*don't do as I do, do as I say*"? Even as an adult, there are some things you just cannot do—you know what I'm talking about. Our children are our messengers, and we need to send them out into the world with a positive message.

It works best if the hero/role model is from your own family.

I want to be that hero for my children. I don't want some model or TV star to be my daughter's role model, I want it to be me. After all, who needs Wonder Woman when you've got your mama?

I wanted to be a hero to my boys too, in a different way. On Mother's Day one year, Andre gave me a card he made in school that depicted me as Super Mommy. I loved that card. I guess I wanted to be the one to burst through walls and leap over tall buildings and big kitchens to do the right thing for my kids. I wanted to let them know the sky was the limit for their aspirations. Along with all that bursting and leaping, I still have the responsibility to carry myself as a respectable parent.

I know my children did not have to look at fictional heroes for good examples. A real-life hero sat at the head of the dinner table every night at our house. He was their father, Julius Rock. His dedication and commitment to his family was a powerful model for all our children. He came home every Thursday and put his paycheck down. He made sure everything went well in our house. We never worried when Daddy was in the house. Just his presence made us feel we were OK and nothing could be wrong as long as he was there.

Be a Mama Rock from the Block

There will be times when you are called to outside duty. My Kenny told me I was the extra *mama* for lots of kids on our block. He said our family values influenced some of his friends—even to this day. Whenever you get a chance, be a *Mama Rock from the*

An excellent resource for any parent is the Big Brother and Big Sister Clubs of America (BBBS). This organization helps children of all ages, races, and religions all over the country. BBBS has volunteer mentors ("Bigs") involved in one-to-one mentoring matches with children ("Littles") in thousands of schools across the country. It is one of the largest in-school volunteer forces in the nation's history. Call on them—that is why they exist.

block. Offer guidance and be a good role model to any child who needs it. There are never too many good mamas.

It's important for single parents to find a role model of the opposite sex for their children. No matter how committed and dedicated you are as a parent, I know you could use some help. If your own parents are good examples, use them. You can also reel in a brother, sister, cousin, in-law, or family friend to serve in that capacity. Otherwise, find a coach or teacher who will have great influence. It really does take a village of mamas, daddies, brothers, sisters, grandparents, and members of the community to raise a good child. Call on whomever you need, and be someone who is needed whenever you can.

All that aside, no matter what, as a parent you are the role model—good or bad. How you set examples in your behavior every day (in every way) determines your child's perspective. Hey, I never said it was easy. You may have to clean up your act and fly right.

MAMA'S MOJO Get your child's input about whom they consider a role model outside the home. Ask them why they look up to this person. You will learn a great deal

from that discussion. It may shock and surprise you,
but it's a start down an important path.

To Keep a Balance, Check and Recheck

It's a good idea to keep a system of checks and balances on your kids, just like the government. While I don't suggest you monitor your children 24/7, you will regret it if you don't know what's going on before someone rings your doorbell with news you don't want to hear.

It's a tough world out there with a lot of pressure for a teenager. I happened to be walking outside near a Manhattan Catholic high school at the end of a school day. Some of the young girls had hiked up the skirts of their modest uniforms and tied their shirts at the waist. The girls pulled some sexy shoes out of their backpacks and slipped them on. Then, off they went. I guess they felt safe because no parent was scheduled to come along at a certain time.

And, how about kids who go to the mall to be with whomever they want? Tricky teens sometimes use a decoy pal who gets in the car on the way to mall, but after they get there, they split up and hang out with others you don't know about, including that one bad influence a parent doesn't want near her child.

If I walked up on my child at the mall and she was with John instead of Stephanie, I would start in with questions like: "Where is Stephanie?" If the answer is not good enough, I'd say: "Let's call Stephanie's cell phone"—you do have your children's friends' cell phone numbers, don't you? This kind of thing goes on all the time.

The point is, you can stop your child if he never knows when you might show up. After all, who says you didn't happen to remember something you needed at JCPenney in the mall on the same day your daughter planned to be there?

> MAMA'S MOJO There are times when—every once in awhile—you should show up after school. Be casual. Say you took a late lunch and thought you'd swing by to take your child home. Even if you do it just that one time, your child will never know when you might do it again (or where). He won't be sure, so that should keep him straight for quite awhile.

Andi was walking with friends in the mall one day. Her girlfriend told her she saw a lady coming the other way who looked just like me. I was close enough to hear Andi loudly say: "Oh Lord, you are right, it is my Mama." When I walked over, she said the same thing she always did when I'd walk up on her somewhere: "Uh-oh. Here she comes, *Big Rose* came to town, look out." She might laugh, but I'm sure she got the message.

> MAMA'S MOJO Now listen, are you going to let your kids snub you? Do they get all huffy and annoyed if you show up at the mall, for instance? What? Are you going to not check up on them so they will "like" you? Where's your head? It's much more important for your child to respect you and your judgments than to be your buddy. How many times do I have to say this?

Every Action Has a Reaction

Everything has a consequence, good or bad. If you say no, mean it. Kenny always said I was tougher than his father about discipline. True, but Julius and I were a tag team and we didn't back down. Don't let your kids get between you and your spouse. Any indecision can be viewed as permission for your children to do whatever they want (you never officially said no). Use the phrase "I'll tell you later," if both parents/caregivers can't agree on a decision at the moment. Be sure to tell them later, too.

How come so many parents just give it up? Honestly, it's because it is easier to say yes than to say no. It's much simpler to let your children go somewhere on their own—even if you aren't sure it's the right thing—than it is to plan an activity together or spend time at home. Some parents think it's more pleasant than having to deal with sulks or tantrums.

> MAMA'S MOJO Nobody ever died from crying or pouting. Who cares if your kid sulks? Don't be afraid of his reaction to your actions. If he wants to huff and puff and blow the house down, he is going to have to do it behind closed doors in his own room. Get him out of your sight—and away from TV and computers. If you're stumped on what to do, send him to his room until you can think of appropriate consequences.

I'll never forget one time when Andi told me she needed a black skirt and white blouse for the school band. After work, I took her over to Wal-Mart to look for the clothes. She announced how she didn't want anything from Wal-Mart, only from Belk Department Store. We got back in the car and I kept driving right past Belk. She wanted to know where I was going. "Listen," I said, "you asked me for what you wanted, and I took you where I was planning to buy the outfit. You decided you didn't want it. Therefore, we're going to shop in your closet instead." She wore what she already had and never pulled anything like that on me again.

Pull Out That Can of *Whup-Ass*

Sometimes children learn consequences for bad behavior all by themselves. Most of the time, though, we parents have to take care of delivering those consequences. Chris likes to say I know "100 kinds of *whup-ass*." Let me be real clear: my *whup-ass* expands far beyond just a physical punishment. It's about whatever I can do to change a negative behavior. It is about taking something away from a child and how he feels about it. Believe me, I've got a lot of tricks up my sleeve for making that happen. I can unleash *whup-ass* disciplinary techniques like nobody's business. Even the threat of opening a can of my *whup-ass* will have just the right psychological effect on my kids. It takes clear action, sometimes, to let your child know who is in charge. I still rely on my mystery can of *whup-ass* because no one knows what it's going to be until the lid is already off and they have to face the consequences.

One time, my son Charles, "Shabazz," bought fireworks for his brothers before the July 4th holiday. Chris could not resist the temptation of those rockets sitting in the corner of his room; he launched a giant Roman candle out of the upstairs window around dinnertime. It flew by our neighbor's head. Still upstairs, he watched the angry neighbor run across the street toward our home.

Apparently, Chris ran downstairs to greet the fuming fellow on the stoop outside. He put on a shocked, wide-eyed look as he listened to the man's story. Chris informed the man about the awful tenant upstairs who did this thing all the time with fireworks. That seemed to work until later, when the neighbor discovered the truth—we didn't have any tenants. Chris ended up with no TV privileges, games, or friends over for two weeks.

And sometimes your children can learn the lessons alone. For example, Chris landed his first big job on *Saturday Night Live*. After all his struggles, here was the big paycheck. He ignored some basics about money management. He immediately bought a fancy new sports car. After he insured it, he was flat broke. That woke him up better than any money lecture I could give.

No matter what the actual action you use in your house, you need to be consistent about enacting consequences for breaking the rules. Set it up beforehand. If you are stumped, send your child into another room (without privileges) until you can think of something. Be sure to say you'll come up with something *really soon*. Most times, the anticipation of an open can of *whup-ass* is worse than the final punishment.

Know When to Lighten Up

Don't punish for every infraction. If you lay the right groundwork, you can choose your battles wisely. Some actions are only childish mistakes or just plain accidents—they are not intentional. I've seen kids hurry to cover their faces after they have spilled a glass of milk at school. Who in the world would hit a child for spilling milk accidentally? Sometimes you have to laugh about the mishap and say, "Ohmigod!" One time Tony broke our window when he hit a home run from way down the street. What a hit! Wow! I said, "Omigod!"

Another time, Tony and Andre accidentally turned over a gallon of bright yellow paint in my kitchen on the floor. They looked over at me in absolute horror. We all looked at that bright paint all over the place and burst out laughing. We laughed until we cried. Then, we cleaned up every single drop.

They shouldn't have been roughhousing indoors—but it was not intentional. I didn't call them a bunch of dumb idiots or lose my cool. Instead, as a family, we cleaned it up. Let me tell you, I was so grateful we got it up off the floor or else I'd have had to paint the entire kitchen yellow.

Let the Punishment Fit the Crime

Don't use overkill like removing all privileges for two weeks over a minor offense like not doing the dishes. Make a punishment appropriate, fair, and immediate. After all, the purpose of consequences for kids is to learn from them and change—not be so ticked off that later they will let their own kids do anything.

Most often, severe, inappropriate, or utterly ridiculous punishments are applied during a moment of fury. Your child is NOT really going to stay in his room all summer, is he?

> **MAMA'S MOJO** When you don't have a consequence, ask your child what HE thinks is an appropriate consequence. Yes, ask. My kids always offered worse consequences than I would have given out. It's worth doing this because they are going to be punished anyway—you are just giving them a hand in their own punishment. Doesn't that seem fair? Of course it does. Use this and you will give the impression of being fair.

Don't Ask a Yes or No Question

I want to share with you one of the most important things I learned in parenting. *NEVER* ask a yes or no question, especially when it relates to crime and punishment. Don't say, for instance, "Did you break that cabinet door?" Forget it; you'll never find out because the answer will always be no. Nobody knows "nuthin," ever.

If no one comes forward to discuss a mess, wait a day or two. Then, let your children think you already know what's going on. Sit down with the suspected culprit over a bowl of ice cream or have some cookies together—nice and casual. Phrase your question like this: "**When** you did this (broke the lamp or piece of china) were you bouncing a ball or did you throw it around the room with someone else?"

Pick Your Battles, Don't Gum It Up!

My older sons love to talk about their self-proclaimed *statutes of limitations* every time we get together. The statutes refer to secret happenings around the house or the family, which we parents didn't know about until long after the fact—sometimes years afterward.

The statutes would often be their own justice system. It was their way of handling sibling in-house bickering or minor fights in school. As the oldest, Chris shouldered much of the responsibility of "not telling" or taking care of the problem in-house without us. Chris, Andre, Brian, and Tony were the early band of brothers who didn't get each other in trouble with Mama. They also learned that tattling was not the way to go unless it was something important. (Tony likes to say Kenny and Andi slept through the Rock justice system because by the time they were eligible, Julius had passed away and the dynamics had changed.) Sometimes they'd cover up for somebody who lost some money or flubbed up somewhere. Some things took awhile to find out—but we always eventually found out. One example was the tale of the bubble-gum machine.

We had an antique bubble-gum machine (with real gumballs) in our house on Decatur Street in Brooklyn. It was an interesting piece with a heavy wrought-iron bottom. The coin slot still worked. We kept it stocked with gumballs and the boys got to keep the change if any visitors put in money. Later, we moved it upstairs to the game room area. But then it disappeared. Of course, no one knew anything about it. The *statutes of limitations* must have expired at some point because—years later—I finally found out what happened.

My husband always putted golf balls around the house—he got on my last nerve about it, too. Following his lead, the boys went one further and chipped the balls. Well, I guess one of those balls headed straight for the old glass gum dome and shattered it. The boys took it apart, cleaned up the gum and the glass, and never said a word. They were ingenious about it, too. The machine pieces were snuck out inside a coat, one by one, under cover of night. Thank God it wasn't a body. I didn't make a stink about it—sometimes you have to pick your battles.

> **MAMA'S MOJO** The bottom line is: kids are kids and boys are truly boys. You never want to totally zap that spirit, browbeat them, or pound them down so they are no longer special.

Always look for the *teachable moments*. Never let one pass. Sometimes kids come in from school and talk about different things that happened—someone got in trouble for badmouthing a teacher, had a fight, found out a friend was a liar. All these are important. Use them to reinforce your rules and beliefs.

Remember, above all, the key thing you can do for your children is to spell out exactly what you expect from them. Don't be all talk and no action—follow through on what you say and be a good role model to your children.

It's not possible to be a pal and an enforcer at the same time. As a parent, you need to win the authority game by letting your children know who is in charge. Help them understand that their behavior is a matter of choice—look for the intention in their actions. We'll explore more about the surprising truth of discipline and why children really long for structure.

A tree is known and recognized and judged by its fruit.
—Matthew 12:33

Remember Mama Rock's Rules and Strategies

■ **Draw the Line to Win Respect**
 You can't be both parent and friend to a child. You need to be a winner in the authority game—the stakes are higher than you think.

■ **Don't Hide the Cookie Jar**
 Help kids understand how behavior becomes a matter of choice. Don't forbid the cookies in the jar—just show kids how to get them without fear.

■ **Join the Congregation of Expectations**
 The most important thing you can do for your children is to set down exactly what you expect from them.

- **Don't Just Set the Table: Set a Good Example**

  Be your child's role model by carrying yourself in the right way—children need to find their best hero in their own home.

- **Every Action Has a Reaction**

  You can't be wishy-washy about your response because you are hurried, tired, or fed up. React consistently each time.

- **Pull Out That Can of *Whup-Ass***

  It takes clear action to let kids know who is in charge. Store some cans of whup-ass *in your pantry to change negative behaviors.*

- **Sometimes You Have to Break the Rules**

  Pick the battles to reinforce your rules and beliefs. Don't browbeat your kids so they no longer feel special—remember, children are children and boys are truly boys.

2

No Child Really Wants to Be Left Alone

IT IS UP TO US to make our children feel protected and secure by creating structured boundaries. We need to let them know we care enough to set the rules. Children without rules may boast of being free from the "sissy" or "stupid" rules their friends have to follow. Yet, deep inside they long for some kind of structure and don't want to be left alone. They wish someone cared enough about them to put dinner on the table each night, or at least leave a meal in the fridge ready to heat up. They want a parent to check on their homework, see if their clothes are clean, or insist they keep in touch when they are away from home.

All children want to feel cared for in those ways, no matter what they say. It frees their energy for other things if they are not worried about what's going to happen next—all the time—because there is no structure in their lives.

Do the Math: More Structure = Better Discipline

I've seen children come home from school an hour or two before a parent. They will drop their schoolbooks and run around the block with no structure, no chores, no one to report to, and nothing to do. More often than not, those kids get into some kind of trouble. If something happens while they run around—like an accident or a fight—they are at the mercy of the neighborhood. If kids know where they have to be and what is expected of them, they don't have as much time or reason to get into trouble.

Brian: It was an irony growing up in our family. Many times, I felt rule-bound because others seemed so free. But now I know those "free souls" suffered a lot. I know because some of them have told me so.

My formula is simple: *more structure for your kids creates less trouble and less need for discipline.* Rules and routines help your kids know what to do without being told repeatedly. This especially holds true for chores, schoolwork, and bedtime. A clear expectation of a child's behavior tells him what he must do to stay on your good side.

Lack of structure brings stress and confusion. This could be why some kids do what they do—like stay out all night and other risky behaviors—just to get the attention they crave and to lower their stress.

Andi once called me one night from South Carolina when I was in New York to tell me about her plan to go to the Huddle House restaurant that evening. Of course, I wouldn't have known where she was. She said, "Ma, I need to tell you where I am going tonight, I just do." I guess she needed that old, familiar feeling of reporting to Mama (even though she was too far away to hear me say, "Andi, is that you?" when she came in that night).

The best way to get kids to internalize discipline is to be consistent in your expectations of them. For example, if you are running downstairs to the laundry room (or anywhere not right next to your kids), begin your expectation requests. Spell out the rules clearly like this: "I expect you kids to sit down on the couch and color in your coloring books (or any passive activity) and stay there. I'll be back in a flash."

When you get back, if they behaved, compliment them. Stay consistent as you build a sense of behavior expectations in your kids; it becomes a natural process that way. By the time it is appropriate to leave them home alone for awhile, they've learned what to do (and not to do). You can't just pick up and leave your kids alone.

> **MAMA'S MOJO** If you can't be there when they get home, spell it out with a note or tell them at breakfast to expect a certain snack in the fridge in the afternoon

when they get home. Assign a few chores like sweeping the
kitchen floor. After that, make clear it will be time to do
homework until you return. Leave no guesswork and
your children will be safe and secure in the
confines of your house. }

When you create consistency in your structure and discipline,
you will create self-discipline in your child. That's what you want
to instill in your child—to be successful in this life, not just when
he is home alone.

Build Up Your Kids with Structure

Don't give me that garbage either about how structure and rules
squash a child's creativity or the ability to become independent.
We had a house full of rules, and my kids are as creative and independent as anyone, each in a different way.

There are even ways to use rules that help develop creativity.
For instance, when I was a teacher, I always made sure my lesson
plan included a one-hour "free play" first thing in the morning. It
meant children could choose among the art, water games, or the
musical instrument tables. That way, each child was allowed the
freedom to choose—within a structured situation—the first experience of the day. He could be free, flexible, and creative within
a controlled environment.

It's not a mystery. Structure is all about order. After all, there
is an order to everything. Without some kind of structure, every-

body would be aimless at home, at the job, or in the classroom. How could anyone know when and where to be and what must be done? Think about it; it's basic! If your child doesn't learn to respect the basic structured rules at home, there isn't much of a chance he can relate to class rules, or later, the rules of the workplace. Then, stop and think again about this: if your child respects your rules and the values they represent, he will be more apt to give respect to teachers and other authority figures. He will be able to "play by the rules" to go after and achieve his dreams.

As long as you set up appropriate rules to create a structure, you can offer your children some independence and confidence—you can even teach them to be on time. For example, when my kids were young, students were allowed to leave the school campus during lunch. Sometimes, the kids rode the bus or train to school. Andi walked the five blocks to school from kindergarten through second grade with her friends (there was a crossing guard at every corner). So, I armed the kids with plenty of basic safety rules, like: don't stand on the edge of a subway/train platform because someone might try to push you, or wait until the train (or car or bus) fully stops before you walk around—those kinds of things. So, with those rules in mind, Chris could go across the street to get a McDonald's meal for lunch and get back to school in time. Tony and Andre could come to the house at noon for a pizza sometimes. Although things aren't as easy today, there are still good guidance rules you can give your children, which allows them to experience independence (like my kids did)—and the chance to be more confident.

The House Rules "Safety FIRST" Section

Don't Open the Door for Uncle Jerome

Before anything else, parents, you have to be ready with your safety rules in place as early as possible. Make sure your kids can understand and follow them. One way to keep a child confident about the time when he will be alone is for him to know he is safe because your family has planned his security and he understands the rules. He is prepared to take charge and be independent, first in small ways and later on his own.

First, establish a set of house rules for times when the kids are alone. This doesn't only mean when you go out for the evening; it includes when you are just in the laundry room, down the hall, in the study, or in the bathroom for a few minutes.

I've gone over to people's houses when the children have answered the door while the mother was out in the backyard. I've had to say, "Please close the door while you get her and I will wait outside." Otherwise, the kids were going to leave the door wide open and walk away to get their mother.

I guess I stressed the house rule *Don't Ever Open the Door* (except for the pizza man—because we knew him—and then lock it afterward) too strongly. While I was out one day, my brother-in-law, Jerome, stopped by, knocked on the door, and called my name. Chris and Andre came to the door because they recognized his voice. The boys told him (through the glass) how sorry they were, but their mama told them not to open the door for anyone. He told the kids he'd wait for me on the stoop.

When I drove up a few minutes later and heard the story, we laughed. Even though Jerome was miffed at first, he said it was "the greatest thing" how my kids listened so well to the rules.

The same holds true for phone calls. Don't ever have your kids say, "Mama's not home." Tell them to say, "She can't answer the phone now, please call back." If it's important enough, they will call back. You'd think everyone would know that, but they don't.

One time Andre met one of my neighbors at our front door. He asked Andre to get Julius for him. "Daddy's in the shower," Andre said. The neighbor then asked if he could talk to me. Andre said, "Mama's in the shower with Daddy, so you can't see her either." After that, we had to tell him to think twice about what he told people. It is best to teach the kids to say someone in the family is not available *at the moment* and take a message.

Another thing: if your child walks to school, be sure there's no name visible on his clothing or backpack. Teach kids not to offer other information, especially to a person asking directions from a car. Hey, tell them not to get close to anyone in a car. For crying out loud, tell your kids not to brag to anyone about plans to be home alone. Kids do it when it isn't even true. It is asking for trouble either way.

Teach the "911" Talk Today!

Let's start out with a few basics. Just because you instruct your child to call an emergency number like "911" doesn't mean he will know what to say. Tell him when and why to call.

As soon as possible, teach your children to memorize their addresses, phone numbers, and their parents' full names. How many kids think a mother's name is *mama* or a father's name is *daddy*? Do your kids know your whole name, where you work, your cell phone or pager number? If not, you know what to do now.

Don't Wait for an Emergency

Emergency plans are a family priority. Fire can be a deadly, rapid killer. Make a fire plan for how everyone could get out of the house. If you don't have a smoke detector, go get one, don't wait.

The beauty of our house now is that anyone who is upstairs can get out of his or her window in case of emergency. Even so, we go over other evacuation scenarios and what we would do if they happened. Make a chart and hang it on one of the walls to tell visitors and the kids' sleepover friends exactly how to exit the house. Don't forget to share *your* plan with overnight guests.

Teach the kids this: if they smell smoke or hear the smoke alarm, get the hell out of the house—that's why you pay for homeowner's insurance. Don't stop to look for anything. My kids know if they smell smoke downstairs, they should go right out the front door. If they see smoke upstairs, they know to go to the roof from their windows. From there, they will go down to the grass and meet at our prearranged place.

Always designate a safe house or area for the family to meet. Make sure it's easy and everyone knows where it is (including guests). Everyone needs to know ahead of time where to meet so that if anyone gets separated, he knows where to go.

> **MAMA'S MOJO** Pick a "safe house" in the neighborhood. Be sure to check if your neighbor is OK with being the "safe house." After all, it might be 2 A.M. when a family meets there during an emergency. Once everyone arrives at the safe house, it is easy to figure out who is missing and find him or her. Even at a theme park, for example, pick a place like the cotton candy booth. That way, if anyone gets lost you know to meet up there, and you know what you can snack on while you are waiting for someone to show up.

Strangers Aren't the Only Danger

It's a tough subject to bring up, but it must be discussed. Those who might harm your child are often people they know, like, and respect. I never believed in a separation between *strangers* and *people we know* when it comes to helping your child to be cautious and aware of appropriate adult behavior. It's not easy to teach a child who is bad—sometimes the bad guy is not who we might think it is.

What you can do is teach appropriate behavior boundaries for adults and children. Help them learn the red flags to watch out for. If you do that, they can recognize inappropriate words or actions, even if the adult involved is a favorite teacher at school or the father of a friend. Let your kids know, above all, to always tell you what is going on. Emphasize why secrets about questionable behavior are not secrets to keep—especially if someone told them not to tell us parents about what went on.

Don't you, as a parent, be a stranger to anyone who regularly comes into contact with your child. It is helpful to know everybody. Be sure to meet the custodian, the cafeteria cooks, the crossing guard, and, of course, your child's teacher at school. It doesn't hurt for them to know you are so-and-so's mama, either. They will probably keep an eye out for your child because of it, too.

> MAMA'S MOJO Take the time to meet your child's teacher as soon as you can. A teacher will naturally pay more attention to your child when he or she has met a parent. It helps to add an extra layer of support to your child's school success.

Get to know who is in charge if your child is picked up at day care or is a car rider at school. Make sure the most current names are on the permission list. If anything changes in your household, update your permission lists immediately. You don't have to list relatives (next of kin or not) if you don't feel completely secure about having them spend time with your child in an emergency or if you are delayed by traffic.

Kids Long to Belong

Rules and routines feel safe to children. They know their boundaries and what is expected of them. You've probably seen a group of kids playing outside until, one by one, each is called to join the family for dinner. There's usually at least one child—maybe two—whom no one has called inside. It is the same story when teenagers hang out in the mall. Right about the time curfews kick in as parents come by to pick up their children, take a close look at the ones who are left behind. They might swagger about with false bravado, but if you look hard, you can see the "longing to belong" look in their eyes. They want that feeling of knowing where they need to be and what they need to be doing.

Most of these kids have to hook a ride home. Even after they get there, parents might not be around or may be too preoccupied to have any thought about what's best for their child. Believe me, a child aches for someone to care enough to make him come home and be in bed by 10 P.M. so he can be ready for school. Kids need someone to care about their well-being.

Tony told me it always made him feel good to know I was waiting up when he came back home at night: "Mommy didn't sleep, I don't think she ever did until we were all home. I'd come in late and she'd call out 'Tone? Is that you?' I'd answer her and she'd ask a question or two about my evening, then she'd go to sleep. I can't imagine a child who goes in and out of the house and nobody ever checks if he is back and in bed or how it went."

One of my son's good friends lived near us on the block. His mother had a great job but took no daily responsibility for her preteen. She gave him a food allowance each week. When my kids came inside for lunch or dinner, he'd go down to the corner store to buy sandwiches or junk food and bring it back to the stoop. He ate his meal and sat there until my boys came outside to play again.

He never accepted our offers to join us for dinner. Maybe his mother told him not to go to anyone's house for a meal. It was heart-wrenching to see him there. What mama would not cook for her child, even if she had to leave a meal for him to heat up at home because she would not be there?

The Curfew Capers

I tried to give my boys a "heads up" when it was almost time to come back into the house for dinner. Sometimes children have trouble switching from one thing they are doing to another. So, I'd call out: *"You got 15 minutes!"* Although Andre and Tony would make it back in time without question, Chris would drag back reluctantly. He began to question our rules. He'd ask me: "Why can't I stay out? Other kids are still out there." It was time for one of my *"mama knows the future best"* speeches: "The day will come," I said, "when you are going to leave Decatur Street and go out on your own. You'll come back sometime and those same kids who sit on the stoop will still be here, sitting on the stoop, I promise you that."

Late one night, years later, Chris flew into JFK Airport. He picked up his car (this was pre-limo days) and decided to go through the old block on the way to his apartment. As he drove down Decatur Street, he actually saw two of those neighbor-hood guys still sitting on the same stoops, even at that late hour.

When he got to his apartment, he called me. "Ma," he said, "remember how you told me those kids sitting on the stoop would always be sitting there? You were right, Ma, they are still there. I saw them tonight!" He was so amazed, he had to call me to say I was right about those guys. It made a big impression.

> MAMA'S MOJO Perhaps I should put a sign behind my house: "*Madame Mama, Child Psychic.*" Sure, most mamas could put that sign up, too. We know just what the future holds for our children if they don't follow our rules. Why do you think we can tell them about it ahead of time?

The Real Deal on C.U.R.F.E.W.

I've never known of a child who begged for a curfew. Too often, curfews end up being a power struggle between parents and teens. But curfews are part of caring for your child. Even teenagers still need boundaries. Ally had a surprising perspective. She recently told me why she loved the curfews and boundaries when she lived in the Rock house. It made her feel "accounted for and protected," she said. She knew if she stepped out of line, we were coming to get her. However, if she got lost or was in trouble, we'd come to get her just the same. She would never be left alone in our family. Like Ally said, kids want to know someone is watching out for them—even if they don't want to admit it.

Here's an easy way to set up and enforce curfews:

C = **Confirm** with all the kids before they leave the house:
(1) where they are going and how they are going to get there, (2) whom
they are going with, and (3) what time they need to come home.

U = **Understand that curfews are not for the convenience of your child.**
Decide upon the consequences of breaking curfew long before your
child ever goes out.

R = **Remember to reinforce consequences** ahead of time if curfew rules
are broken. Be specific. For example, tell your child: "Tonight your
curfew is 11 P.M. If you are going to be late, you must call. Unless it is
an emergency, if you are more than twenty minutes late, you will be
grounded."

F = **Forget a standardized curfew time** for every child. There can be
different curfews for different activities, including special events at
work and school (like prom night or a football game). Decide what time
works best for your family, an individual child, or your community.
(Remember, some local areas have their own curfews for kids under a
certain age.)

E = **Enforce the consequences** if curfew is not followed. Use such situations to teach the need for responsibility.

W = **Welcome the chance to give your teenager something to work toward.**
When your child honors his curfew, you can award him more privileges
(like a later curfew). It is a good chance to build a sense of responsibility.

Don't Be at a Loss for Who Is Boss

Single parents need to keep their family rule structure in place, especially if they suddenly become single. I had already become a single parent when I moved with three young children to South Carolina from New York after the death of my husband.

Those were hard times, even for little things. I didn't know cars didn't come filled with gas until after Julius died. I had been in a marriage where so much was taken care of for me. With death or divorce, many of us have to take charge of things we never had to do before. And children will continue to test limits—especially curfew limits—at a time when we are least emotionally equipped to deal with it all.

This is the thing: as a single parent you have to reinforce your rules even more because no one is there to back you up or pick up the slack. Step up to the game (especially if you are raising boys) to let them know the rules must continue to be followed. Impress on them that you still call the shots—yes, just you—because even alone, you remain the boss. It is an uneasy time for everyone. The script has changed, but you can help your children feel safe by being consistent.

Be There If You Care

All kids want to know they matter to someone. They want to know they are important to you by the way they are received when they need you. It would be wonderful if each child had at least one adult in his life who put him ahead of everything, who was madly in love with him; one person—a parent would be ideal—who lights up when he walks in the door.

Ally pointed out something I never noticed until she said it. During meals, she observed, I'd focus completely on each child as I dished out each individual plate for dinner. She remembered how I'd look straight at each one to ask a preference—"Do you want an extra roll? Salad? Did you say no to the beans? What else would you like?" As it turned out, each child experienced my complete personal attention in a room full of family. It helped them settle down to dinner and feel loved and appreciated. I still do that when I serve a meal, even with my grown-up children. Only now I know how much it matters to them.

Jordan asked me recently why I still don't sit down until everyone is served. I told him I don't sit down until my children are all set with their meal. It is my way to show love.

Don't Be Too Busy to Be Bothered

Sometimes you see children alone or without anyone from their family in attendance at the school play, concert, or game because a parent is too "busy." I don't care what kind of high-powered job you have; you can get away for an hour (skip your lunch hour or stay late) to be somewhere important to your child. When I say make time for something important, I don't mean only if it is your child's graduation or she is the star of an HBO special. Even if your youngster has one line in a class production, you need to care enough to be there. Unconditional love—which is so important to a child's development—is needed during the growing-up years. Later, when a child must rely on himself, he will draw from it for personal strength and resilience.

Once, my foster daughter, Jennifer, was in a play at school on a busy day for me. She asked over and over if I'd be there. I knew it was important to her, so I went into work and pulled whatever I could to get myself to her event.

When I walked in and sat down, she was already on stage. I could tell she was looking around for me, so I stood up. When she saw me, her face just opened up with happiness. She turned around and performed her role with great energy. Foster children often think that if you don't show up, they are not as important as the other children; so it was even more crucial that I made the time. Jennifer's look of pure joy was enough reward for me.

{ **MAMA'S MOJO** Even if you are all ready to go out, set your handbag down and listen up if your child has something important to talk about. Explain that you have to leave soon, but you want to hear what he has to say. Believe me, your kid will feel like a million bucks. Most times, such discussions take far less time than you think and mean far more than you might imagine. }

Give Your Kids Enough Frequent-Flyer Points

Everything a good parent does prepares their children for that day when they stand on their own. You can give them wings, but you must also teach them to fly—just make sure it is not too soon. If you've prepared your children well, they can cope with any obstacles on life's long runway.

Some parents leave their kids unsupervised much too young, or without enough preparation or rules. We see the consequences of that in the papers every day. There was a recent story about a boy under fourteen whose parents went to New York and left him in the house by himself all weekend. My question was: why on earth didn't they take him along? What could they be doing that was so important? A neighbor happened to find out about it, thank goodness, before it might have been too late. Listen, most parents who walk out of their house and leave a child who is not ready already know they shouldn't do it.

Look at the Bigger Picture

Who is minding the kids these days? The U.S. Census Bureau—the last time I checked—has on record over 600,000 five- to eight-year-old children who are left home alone (at least among those who told the truth to the Census Bureau). Another 3.4 million children are under the care of their young brother or sister.

The foster system has gotten bigger because of all these little kids left alone at home.

New York was always known for loads of latchkey kids—the ones with the key to their front door on a chain or ribbon hung around their neck. Now, it's prevalent all over the country. In some rural areas, mothers get on buses to ride to service jobs in the hospitality industry before their children get up in the morning. They often don't return home until late in the evening. Every neighborhood is in need of a good, reasonably priced after-school program. So many parents have to work two jobs just to make ends meet—what's left for child care? It is a national dilemma. Some parents have been known to lock their kids in at home and pray that all is well, because they have to work and can't afford any day care. There's much more I'm sure we don't know.

Not so long ago a grandmother, cousin, or someone from the extended family was usually available to help. They even wanted to do it! If a worn-out mother needed a break, Grandma could come and watch the kids while Mom took a walk. If someone had to work, a family member was usually a reasonable or no-cost babysitter. As families scatter throughout the country, less support is available and the options are limited.

What's a parent to do? Try to partner with someone who has older children, if yours are young, and get together with other moms to share the cost of a sitter. Be sure to use clear, strong rules when you get a group organized to provide a safe haven for your kids when you cannot be there.

Another thought? Try the barter system to exchange services with other mothers. If you can cook a meal or organize a file cabinet, someone will pitch in and help with your kids in exchange for so much less than the cost of a babysitter. Be creative!

It's Not Just an Age Thing

There are times when you can leave your child home alone safely—and a time when a child is ready to be alone. House rules are so important because children don't always make the best decisions when they are calm, and certainly can't be expected to make good choices under stress. Actually, how well your child handles the unexpected is a good indicator to use in deciding when he can be left by himself.

Anyway, it's not all about age when it comes to being home alone; it's all about maturity level. I know some six-year-olds who act like they are sixteen and some sixteen-year-olds who are way too immature to be left alone. I do know some ten-year-olds I'd leave for a minute if I had to run to the corner store for milk. You shouldn't do that—but you could if you had to.

Look hard at your kids. Think of how they act and what they say to you about the prospect of being alone *before* you try their solo flight. Do they tell you they're afraid of being alone in the house? Can you count on them to follow the ground rules you have set down? All these things must be taken into consideration. There is no "magic" age when a child can be left alone. Each child is different. As a parent, you have to be the one to make that important decision. The National SAFEKIDS coalition recommends no child under twelve years old should be left alone.

Most "home alone" trials begin when a child is around fourteen or so. He doesn't want to tag along with you and feels he is much too old for a sitter. That's a good time for a try-out. Start with an hour's test run. See what happens when you are gone. Now, if you have any hesitation at all, *don't do it.*

When they are ready to be alone, use your head. Don't leave your teenager for the day and say, "Hey, why not fry that chicken up for lunch?" Just because you have a griddle and he's seen you use it doesn't mean he knows how to cook with it. Whatever you instruct for meals or snacks should not involve any cooking dangers. Try to organize meals that don't involve any cooking at all.

If possible, the best thing to do is to write a check for Domino's Pizza and tell the kids to order. (True, sometimes I've come back and had to ask why they ordered cheesy bread and cinnamon bread plus a super-large loaded pizza or why they ordered Pepsi when I had Coke in the refrigerator—but it's still worth it.)

Although I'd leave my children by themselves before I'd involve another kid, sometimes there are one or two kids who fit right in with your crew. Chris's best friend, Randy, was one of those kids. He was like another son to Julius and me. (Julius even went out and bought an extra bed especially for Randy because he spent the night with us so often.) Make it clear to your kids, a "Randy" can come over—no one else—and *his mother must know that no parents will be at home.* If it is OK with his mother, it is OK with me. Of course, you know there are those kids you don't want over even when you *are* at home.

Naturally, there will be a few hiccups: even Randy got banned for a while after an incident at the house. He and Chris were fooling around. Somehow, Chris crashed into a mirrored closet door that cut into his arm, and the mirror was smashed. The boys had two problems: how to fix Chris's arm, which was bleeding all over the place, and how to explain the broken mirror. Chris's arm was wrapped in a big cloth when we came back, but there wasn't a cloth big enough to hide the damage to the mirror! Randy was sent home and Chris was sent upstairs. Of course, we relented in a few days. Everyone missed Randy and he missed us.

One of the most helpful things you can do is to show your children how to enjoy themselves when they are alone at home—without their friends. Show by example how enjoyable it is to sit down with a good book or puzzle for some quiet time. Explain to them why they don't have to hang on the phone or the computer when they are alone. The ability to enjoy one's own company is an important gift to give your children. Allow them to see their home as a safe haven to relax and explore ideas and activities even if they are by themselves.

Be Your Brother's Keeper

The more children you have, the more you need them to watch out for each other. Julius had it right. When Chris would come in after a fight, he'd tell us what happened. Julius would turn to the other brothers and ask them where they were when this was going down. If they were there, he'd ask what they did to help Chris in this fight. He felt strongly that no sibling should stand by while another was being hurt, threatened, or picked on. We stressed the importance of being responsible for each other.

When the boys played sports outside, one of the brothers always played on the same side as Chris. They stayed close. When they hiked at Highland Park, everyone kept together. The brothers' rule was: no matter how much you might fight with each other, you always have to guard each others' backs.

That went for sisters too. Andre and Tony were playing stoopball with Ally one day. Two young girls came by looking for trouble. Earlier that day, one of the girls had apparently complimented Ally on her braids, but Ally didn't respond the way those troublemaking girls thought she should have. They were itching for a chance to make a scene with Ally. Andre and Tony walked over and stood next to Ally without a word. They looked at the girls sternly. Those girls moved real fast down the block and away from Ally.

In the beginning, we left Chris in charge as the oldest. Being in charge is how a child learns responsibility. Later, as work often took him away, the next oldest would be in charge, and so forth. The sibling in charge was entirely responsible for whatever went on in the house. If someone misbehaved, not only was the perpetrator in trouble but so was the kid in charge.

If Andre lost his mittens, Chris was responsible. Before the kids walked out the door to play, he was supposed to check if they had on a hat. Each child had the responsibility to put mittens and scarves inside a coat sleeve and not to lose them when they came inside. Despite that, all the kids were eager to take on the "Chris position" as the one in charge. I think that's why Kenny said Andi and Jordan escaped the Rock justice system; as the two youngest, they never had to be in charge. Andi does watch out for Jordan (when she's not at school). And Jordan? He just has to watch out for himself. Anyway, in coastal South Carolina we don't often need mittens and hats.

Andre: Chrissy had a lot of responsibility because he was the oldest. Later, it would get passed on down. The one in charge would get in trouble if we did something wrong. I've kept the same formula with my kids; I haven't seen it fail yet. I actually planned that my kids would be born close together so they could grow up like we did.

Sometimes, we were disappointed. Our children had firm rules not to go outside when we were not home. When Julius and I went out to a Diana Ross concert one time, Chris was left in charge. While he was busy on the phone with a girlfriend, Ally, Andre, and Tony snuck out of the house.

We were driving home after the concert and had just turned onto our street when a young child ran out on the road. Julius barely missed her with the car. Guess who the child turned out to be? It was eight-year-old Ally! Julius got out of the car, livid, frightened, and ready to holler. He chased Ally into the house. Andre and Tony had already made a run for it. Everybody got in trouble for that one, especially Chris.

No matter how grown up your children act, kids are still kids. Just because they handled things well on their own for a while doesn't mean they won't get scared another time or goof it up. Keep up your preparation, communication, and compliments to prepare your child to make the right choices whether he is with you, with others, or home alone.

Remember Mama Rock's Rules and Strategies

■ **Do the Math: More Structure = Better Discipline**

Rules and routines leave less time for kids to get into trouble. More structure helps create the goal of less-stressed, self-disciplined children.

■ **Don't Open the Door for Uncle Jerome**

Establish a set of house rules for times when the kids are alone (even for a few minutes while you are out of sight). Remember, strangers aren't the only danger.

■ **Why Wait Until an Emergency?**

Figure out an emergency plan now to prepare your children to make the right, safe choices, especially if they will be home alone. Learn the "911" talk—try the drill before it is ever needed.

■ **Strangers Aren't the Only Danger**

Teach appropriate behavior boundaries and help your child learn to recognize the red flags—even from people your child already knows, likes, and respects.

■ **Kids Long to Belong**

Help your children feel protected by structured boundaries. Let them know they belong because you care enough to set rules.

- **Don't Be at a Loss for Who Is Boss**

  Single parents need to step up their game. Let kids know the rules are still in place. Help them feel safe with your consistency.

- **Be There If You Care**

  Do everything possible to attend meaningful events for your children. It reinforces how important they are. So, don't be too "busy" to care.

- **Give Your Kids Enough Frequent-Flyer Points**

  Don't leave them alone too early or let them fly away too soon.

- **Be Your Brother's Keeper**

  Siblings need to watch out for each other. Responsibility begins at home.

3

Wipe Your Mouth Out Before You Come into the House

MY CHILDREN WERE NOT ALLOWED to curse inside our home—lies were not welcome either. Words that hurt others were also not permitted. All of that negative talk should be cleaned up before anyone comes into my house, or yours.

Swearing is disrespectful to anyone within earshot. It's as if politeness up and died these days. Lord, there's so much swearing in school; the teachers and students seem to be deaf, because they don't even react to it. Not so long ago, men did not cuss in front of a woman. There was even a quaint phrase, "men didn't cuss

Kenny: You could never talk to my mama like somebody on the street—not in our house. You could never talk any way you wanted in our house.

in front of mixed company," which meant when women were around. Hey, men didn't spit on the sidewalk, either, because it was considered rude and vulgar. In those days, a child never raised a voice to a parent, never mind a curse word.

You know, there are kids today who actually tell a parent: "don't tell me what to *f#$&ing* do." (Even in my wildest dreams, I couldn't imagine saying such a thing to my folks or hearing one of my kids say that to Julius or me.) Those kids needed their mouths wiped out long before they could ever disrespect a parent that way. It's too late for that game—they need to be washed down with a hose after something like that.

Most everyone feels uncomfortable around an out-of-control mouth, but the use of profanity can cause damage, literally. Conversations can turn into violent arguments—foul words provoke anger more than you can imagine. Swearing hurts in other ways, too. Cuss often enough or at the wrong moment and there could be trouble at school, on the job, or even with friends and lovers.

How Did You Get Your Mouth to Say That?

If one of your baby's first words is *mf#%$*, you are the one with a problem. You forgot to shut off your own out-of-control cussing in front of your kids. Children repeat what they hear, and they learn from their parents. If those in their environment use profanity all the time, what else could be expected? Curse words should be left outside the door to your home. Respect and honest communication need to be on the inside.

Sometimes, a parent's profanity has become a habit. Habits are hard to break—ask anyone who has tried to quit just about anything. Go cold turkey now. Wipe out your own mouth before you come into your own house. It's your responsibility to be a good example.

> **MAMA'S MOJO** Parents, here's a good way to help quit the bad-language habit: substitute made-up, funny words for curse words. Try to learn some new vocabulary words to replace the lazy, bad ones. Stay calm. It's a good idea anyway, but a lot of cussing is a reaction to frustration. After all, you don't want to pay the price of profanity either.

Lay Off the Fuss if Kids Cuss

Bad language often starts as soon as kids get around other kids—at day care, school, or even at a family reunion. In my time, children stayed at Grandma's house, and she usually didn't curse at all. Today, dirty words become the thing to do because kids and teachers go "ooooh" and carry on when bad words are said. When kids see the attention "mouthing off" receives, they want that notice too.

Parents, don't go crazy over cuss words—they don't deserve all that attention. Be cool, but don't let your kids think cussing is cool. After all, most little kids don't even know what they are saying, and older kids just want to bait you. If you react too strongly, they know how to push your buttons with the flip of a tongue.

I believe religiously in the use of "TIME OUT" to handle a need for discipline. I would rather take a child out of a situation and defuse the problem than take any other course of action. Parents, we need that time too. We need to be able to distance ourselves from the kids and chill out enough not to enact a punishment out of pure anger—you all know what I mean.

Treat vile words like all negative behavior: let your child know you love him—you don't love the words he just used in your house. After all, even the best child leaves the school bus with plenty of choice expressions to try out on you.

Try this game with your kids when your child says a bad word. Forget that old soap thing. Hand your child a tissue and say, "Wipe your mouth out from any bad words *before* you come in our door." Then add, "I know you may have heard that word on the bus or at day care (or from your little cousin), but you cannot say that here." Have the child actually wipe his mouth with a tissue and throw it in the garbage along with the "bad word."

Don't Pay the Profanity Price

Anyone who knows how to communicate well is more likely to be taken seriously. If your child's conversation is a cascade of cussing, respectable people will give him the brush-off. Even if he's not ignored, he will leave a bad impression. You can stop your children from being a disrespected person if you stress this fact of life.

Even with the kind of language Chris uses in his act, I know in my heart it is an act, an act on a stage. I don't know Chris Rock, the act. Who I know is Christopher Julius "Chrissy" Rock, and he's not allowed to cuss in front of me or in my house. No child is allowed to cuss at me or in my presence. That is an important rule, and one that I believe left an impression on all my children.

One time Chris and I were together in Atlanta for his HBO special. We arrived early in the day for rehearsal, so he saw where I was to be seated that evening. During the show, he kept looking in my direction until finally a crewmember had to literally move me out of my seat. Chris couldn't get into his robust act when he saw me—I cramped his style. In the future, he was never told where I would be seated when I attended a performance.

I notice some young people in the rap/hip-hop world casually use the most foul and filthy language. Who wants to see guys with pants down around their ankles or even in evening clothes cuss at each other? Some of the young girls in that crowd have the nastiest mouths in the world yet demand to be treated with respect—who are they fooling? So what if someone is a celebrity or a groupie who wants a position on the "A" list? How about the "A" list of undesirables?

Remember, Shame Is a Dirty Word Too

Humiliation was big in my day. Teachers used it all the time—remember dunce caps? What happened then, at such an impressionable time, stayed with many of us all our lives. About the worst thing you can do to children (or anyone) is allow them to be shamed or humiliated.

Words have the power to both heal and damage. Parents or teachers should not use words deliberately to hurt a child. Once those words are said, they can resonate for a lifetime. Too many children have been emotionally scarred by spiteful or untruthful words. It doesn't matter if it happens at home, in the classroom, the sports field, or anywhere. Shame is a dirty word that needs to be wiped out, period.

When I was going to school in the fifties, teachers who came from less-fortunate circumstances often forgot about their roots once they had "made it." If a child lived in the right place and had good, pressed clothes, these teachers paid positive attention. If not, they often treated their students differently. They could even be harsh and demeaning to those less fortunate.

At our black schools, there was no free or reduced lunch. Most of us brought our lunch. I remember one Thanksgiving when I was in the fourth grade, everybody tried to secure a quarter to pay for a special holiday lunch. If a parent had more than one child, coming up with enough money in those times was really tough. This particular year, my parents didn't have enough to pay for both me and my brother.

On the day of the lunch, it turned out that another student and I were the only ones in our class who couldn't pay. Our teacher walked around the entire morning and rubbed it in. She said, "We'll all be eating turkey and cranberry sauce soon except for poor Rosalie [me] and [the other student]." She mentioned how much she looked forward to lunch—while looking in our direction. Finally, everyone left for the cafeteria, except us. We were left behind, alone, in the classroom.

That depressing day was a turning point for me. I said to anyone who would listen that when I became a teacher, I would be kind to all the neglected and poor kids no matter what. I was going to be sure no child in my class would ever be humiliated like I had been.

When my son Andre became a teacher, I was so proud of how he stuck up for the kids who could not afford a school field trip. He even offered to pay for those who would otherwise have to miss the trip.

> MAMA'S MOJO Because of this continuing situation, a division of our family nonprofit organization, *Rock This 619*, was formed to fund school field trips or events for children who cannot afford them. That division is named *The Julius Rock Memorial Fund*. If your PTA or civic group is looking for a project, I cannot think of a better one than to establish a means of financial assistance to cover field trips and other educational events for those students who are unable to afford them.

Buy Your Kid Some Battle Armor

Things are no different today; teachers and others still use humiliation as a tool. What should you do if your child experiences a degrading situation at school? First, you must intervene right away. Schedule an appointment with his teacher (whom, hopefully, you have already met). Discuss the incident. If it was more than a simple misunderstanding, let the teacher know you are concerned. Tell her you won't stand by while something destructive happens to your child. Let the teacher be on notice.

If the teacher does nothing—blow the whistle. It's time for the principal or other authority figures to stop it. Listen now, any parent is doing a big favor to all the students when such a teacher is put on notice. No coach or instructor should ever use humiliation as a teaching tool. Educators need to realize how much power they have over children, both positive and negative.

At one time, parents couldn't do much because teachers were treated like gods—they were always right. Nobody did anything to that awful teacher who embarrassed me and the other student the day of the Thanksgiving lunch. If that happened today, a parent could call a teacher right away to stop the problem and make it right.

> **MAMA'S MOJO** Your biggest job is to build up your children—let them know how great they are. This helps equip them to deal with whatever comes at them, especially if there are bullies or people who try to humiliate them. A supportive home life fortifies your child for whatever battleground is outside in the world. You put some invisible "armor" on your kids every time you validate how important they are to you. Do it enough and nothing can penetrate that "armor" away from home.

Make sure your children know that they can tell you about their troubles at school. Be there to shore up the troops—don't go AWOL when it counts. You must also let your kids know how to act with respect no matter what—explain why and when to zip their lips and not back-talk a rude teacher. Instead, they need to come home and tell you about it.

Names *Do* Hurt—They Really Do

We repeated something when I was a kid; we just didn't know it wasn't true. It's still chanted today: *Sticks and stones will break my bones but names will never hurt me.*

That old saying is a story without glory and it's just plain wrong! Of course, being called a name won't admit you to a hospital, but words that shame wound deeply and can still hurt years later. After all, broken bones can be fixed, but hurtful words and taunts can cause pain for a lifetime.

I don't care who it is—being humiliated destroys self-esteem. Insults, like name-calling, can create self-doubt that doesn't go away.

Mervin "Spectac" Jenkins told me about an incident he remembers from the seventh grade that influenced his approach as a school principal. His English teacher, over six feet tall, towered over the children. One time, he talked out of turn in her class. She gave him a hateful look and called out loudly to him in front of the whole class: "You are *a ding-dong-bat-dumb-door-knob boy.*" He remembered her taunt word for word. He was too afraid to ever speak in her classroom again. Today, "Spectac" helps teachers understand: once you take trust away from a child, you can't teach that child anymore. If you humiliate a child, learning is compromised.

When a child hears someone tell him he is great at something or that he's handsome or kind, it makes him feel good about himself. What happens if children don't ever hear those things? Or, sadly, if they hear hurtful things every day? When that happens, it's easy for a child to believe those words. It's even worse if a parent hurls verbal abuse. Such kids come to believe they can't do anything right—and they become destructive to themselves or to others in a frantic effort to feel better.

Stop Lying Around

The effort to feel better is often the motivator for kids to cover up their feelings of "not being good enough" with lies. I remember when I was in high school and some of us went shopping to look at prom dresses. One girl told us she bought her dress at some fancy place and it cost a lot of money. Later, we found out she was wearing a hand-me-down gown. It wasn't a harmful lie (it didn't hurt anyone) but it told the truth on her: she had a poor self-image. She thought an expensive store-bought dress would make her a more important person to her classmates.

Many children (and adults) think they are "not enough." They seem to equate where they live or the things they have with who they are. They lie to compensate.

When I was younger, I used to embellish things. I'd kind of add on or make something a bit more than it really was. I learned the best way to stop a lie is to get caught—that stopped me. When you tell a lie you better have a fantastic memory, because once you make something up, you have to keep on going. People can trip you up when you lie because a lie has *nothing to stand on*.

Some foster children make up an entire life. Too often, these kids think something is wrong with them because they are not with their mother or father, even though it is not their fault. They make up something that makes them feel better, even if it is not true at all. There is a bright side to this: if enough positives come into such a life—little by little—the "fake" past becomes a "real" and happy present.

Tell the Truth and Nothing but the Truth

The expectation in my house was simple: we expected our children to tell the truth. No matter what a child did, we parents were there to help—as long as they came to us with the truth. We did not accept lies. Of course, I hoped we had prepared them to tell us if something serious or difficult happened. We would rather find out from them than someone else. We wanted to be told the truth, but there were certain things I didn't know if I wanted to hear. It's a hard call. I told Chris when he was young, "there's nothing you can't tell your

Brian: One of the best things my parents did for us was to make us understand that even if we were wrong (and even if we were going to get in trouble with them), it was better to face up to it than to lie. My Parents' #1 Rule About Lies: **Tell the truth no matter how bad it is.** *They said we could always find a way to make it right together. We had a pretty good understanding of when things were too serious to keep secret because we were protecting another person. Our parents helped us learn why it was better to face the music than for something really bad to happen.*

mother." OK, but I don't think I want my child to inform me, "Mommy, I had sex last night." Usually, it's too much information. Of course, if it was one of our girls, we would want to be up on such a thing.

Because so many lies are for self-protection, a parent should try to create a nonjudgmental atmosphere. Above all, be calm. Come on, it is hard for a kid to 'fess up and come clean. Courtrooms and Congress are full of people who have the same problem! Your child should not feel there is anything he could not tell you. Sometimes, a lie builds up big enough so a child would rather die than tell the truth to a parent—he can become terrified of a parent's disappointment or rage. It is horribly true that some kids would consider suicide as a better way out than confessing what went wrong in their lives.

> **MAMA'S MOJO** Calmly remind your children that you will only be let down for a short time if they lie. Emphasize that it is always better to tell the truth no matter what the consequences. Share with them your confidence that you can work out any problem or situation within the family.

Be sure to give positive support for honesty, even if you must deliver consequences for the actual bad deed. You can always say, "Although I don't like what you told me, I'm so proud you were honest." Doing so will build character and a moral sense in your child—a wonderful attribute for a successful life.

One way you can share the truth about lies is to talk about times when other people lied—we all know *someone* who had a problem with the truth. Bring up someone, especially, who got busted in a lie. Then ask the kids why they think this person told such a bald-faced lie. Your kids' answers should interest you. Maybe they will say he was trying to show off or else something sneaky was going on. Then, ask if he was better off lying or not.

My kids have heard my story of the "Queen of the Whoppers." This lady was someone I worked with. She had a major problem with the truth. It did not matter where any of her coworkers (including me) had dined, shopped, or vacationed—she had been there, or bought that, or done one better.

We got suspicious at one point; how could she afford all these things? So, we planned a "sting operation." My coworkers and I invented a place we had "gone" and carried on about our fabulous, fake location. Just as we suspected, she told us she had been there too (in great detail). When we finally told her we made up the whole thing, I thought she would die of shame. She would have liked to fall through the floor of our office if she could have done it.

I think she was shamed into telling the truth from then on. Think how much better her life would have been if someone had done a "sting" much earlier in her life—like her parents.

Julius and I also discussed at the table those times when we had not told the truth and the regret or penalties we paid because of it. Tell it to the children like a story and keep discussions open about why honesty and trust are so important.

Smoke Out the Liars

Telling lies is another behavior to wipe out before your child comes into the house—and before going out of it too! Although we do not treat liars the way it was done in medieval times—when a lie-teller's pants were actually set on fire—it still lives on in the chant: *Liar, liar, pants on fire*. I know I don't want to smell the smoke or have to carry a portable fire extinguisher to keep my house from burning down, do you?

This is no smoke screen: lies break trust. It is up to adults to be role models of open and honest communications with children. It is a serious, tricky subject, but you can do it.

It is not easy to earn trust, but it is worth so much. If you lie to get away with something, most times you get caught anyway. Why go through all of that? Impress on your kids that if they tell the truth, they won't ever have to worry about getting caught.

I'm not talking about the little kids who don't even know they lie—just like they don't know when they cuss. Little ones don't understand the concept of lying, and mostly it is hard for them to tell the difference.

If a neighbor child brings a toy outside, another child always says, "I have that same thing at my house," even if he doesn't. Or, one youngster says to another, "I'm going to the circus with my father." The other one fires back, "I'm going with my daddy, too." She'll say that even if she does not know her father.

Kids say things like that for pure self-preservation. No one wants to look bad or needy in front of his or her peers. What I'm talking about are the serious whoppers and the sins-of-omission lies (when you leave things out). Oh Lord, my kids were big on that!

> MAMA'S MOJO Don't forget to teach your children how to combine honesty with kindness. If a friend asks an opinion of how she looks after a beauty shop visit, no one has to say, "Girl, you look like a fool." So what if she does? It doesn't help to hurt her feelings. Your child doesn't have to say, "Wow, you sure look beautiful." If a comment is necessary, save face for the person by saying, "That sure is *some* hairdo (or party dress or new couch)." It works— it really does. After all, it IS something.

Let Sins of Omission Bring Contrition

What are the reasons kids lie? Sometimes kids cover up for each other. One kid does something—and they all have their own way—but it is handled in-house. Keeping secrets among brothers and sisters creates a strong bond. However, it's serious business if the secrets hide behavior or circumstances that cause major harm.

A brother catches a brother in some dubious behavior. He says, "You know you are not supposed to do it, and if I ever see you do it again, I'll tell Mama." I feel like some small things should be left among siblings. Hopefully, the thought process goes like this: *my brother did something minor (lost some money at school), maybe it's not an offense I need to tell my mother about. I can*

tell him I know what he did and if he quits doing that or fixes the prob-
lem, I'll be OK with it.

I mentioned earlier about my children's "statutes of limita-tions," which covered the behavior they hid from their father and me. A favorite holiday get-together activity is the recounting of those juicy, secret escapades—that is what most of them were, escapades. Like the broken bubble-gum machine—they weren't serious events, no one got hurt.

My boys didn't have to tell me if a brother was at Mrs. Jones's house even after I said not to go there (after all, Mrs. Jones is an old lady and she did not need my kids buzzing around). However, if one of mine saw their brother or sister at a house on the corner, where people engage in questionable behavior—that is an entirely different story.

If I asked one of my kids where his sister went and he told me she went to Stephanie's house, I believed him. If he knew she actually got into a car and went somewhere off-limits, then his sin of omis-sion could lead to serious trouble. How would we both feel if some-thing awful happened because he didn't tell me the whole story?

There are other consequences. When kids lie, they have to earn back the trust of their family. Jordan did some things he was not supposed to do, and even after I called him on it, he still kept doing it—until he got caught. He betrayed my trust in a big way. So, now, if he asks me for the car to go shopping or wherever, I answer him this way: "Jordan, you proved to me by your behavior that you are not trustworthy. Who took that trust away? You did." If he asks why can't a friend stay over when I go to a concert this weekend, I tell him: "I can't trust you yet. You told me a lie." There is a price to pay for what he did, and he has to understand it. I have confidence in Jordan that he can win back my trust. He knows he can because we all believe in him, but he has to show me he has learned the lesson by sticking with the truth.

Remember, to make it plainly understood: your children must tell you the truth. It is so important to instill respectful and honest communications inside your home—leave the cuss words, lies, and shameful behavior outside the front door.

Remember Mama Rock's Rules and Strategies

- **Don't Pay the Profanity Price**

  Cussing at the wrong time can bring trouble at school and work—it can even bring on violence. Profanity damages in many ways.

- **Shame Is a Dirty Word Too**

  About the worst thing you can do to a child is to allow him to be shamed or humiliated.

- **Buy Your Kids Some Armor**

  Provide your child with the "armor" of your love and positive feedback to win the battles of life.

- **Dispel the Lie: Names Do Hurt**

  Name-calling hurts self-esteem. That "sticks and stones" chant is a story without glory.

- Don't Raise a "Queen of the Whoppers"

   Some people think they are not "good enough," so they lie to compensate. Bring such lies out in the open—if enough positives happen, the fake life can become a happy, real life.

- Tell the Truth and Nothing but the Truth

   Rule #1: Your children must tell you the truth. When they do, they'll never have to worry about being caught.

4

Feed Them and They Will Tell You Everything

L AST YEAR, CHRIS SENT ME a Mother's Day card, which still sits on my desk. It says, "A Son Remembers." Inside the card is a poem about how happy and secure life was around our kitchen table. I'm so thankful Julius and I could give him such joyful memories.

I still miss getting ready for the family dinner each evening. Even with all the commotion and busy work involved, there are moments when I'd give anything to have all my children back as they were, ready for me to serve up dinner. I understand they had to grow up, and I'm proud of them, yet I long for those gatherings. For me—for all of us—it was the best time of the day because we were together. We knew where everyone was. It was great to sit back with Julius and watch the kids laugh and talk. Nobody had to run upstairs or do homework. It was a special family time.

I remember when I was growing up, most families tended to sit down and have dinner together. No matter how meager the fare—my grandmother once said even if it's only "grits 'n grease"—we'd all sit at the table and eat together. It was expected. Besides, what could a parent be doing that is more important than being with a child and eating together? What could be more valuable to a child than spending some nonpressured time with parents, brothers, sisters, and others at the family table?

And so, we made dinner together a major part of the Rock family tradition. We *made* the time to connect. We used it as a chance to listen and to learn about the kids. We were surprised at what we found—even when we didn't look too hard.

Today, you can't seem to pick up a magazine or read a news article about family life without mention of the importance of family meals. Statistics say kids who have meals with their folks are less apt to do just about anything bad—like smoke, drink, get bad grades, or whatever. The family dinner is some kind of cure-all, according to these articles and statistics. Maybe it is. So much is learned at the table, so many bonds are formed; so many confessions and dreams are shared. I think it is the heart and soul of family identity.

Actually, it doesn't have to be a dinner; it could be a family lunch or even breakfast if that's the only schedule that works, as long as the plan is followed. It is a time for everyone to be together, no exceptions. Even though there were at least five siblings running around our house at any one time, no one was allowed to say, "I'll eat in my room," or, "I'm coming down later."

Some statistics say kids eat better at the family table. I know my kids ate better because I was able to see that they ate properly. If the kids were eating somewhere else like in front of TV or in their room, I could never be sure what they were eating and what they might throw away. And, I know my kids ate vegetables because I served a vegetable at every meal. If a child didn't like a vegetable, say turnip greens, I always had a salad available. If you bring out a few dressings and suggest they taste a dressing or two—believe me, the salad gets eaten. The other part is that the children could see us trying out different foods—sometimes I think they would try it just because we set that example by eating it first.

Brian: I don't know if I would ever have understood how powerful a regular family dinner was if I hadn't been part of one. Not everyone was as blessed as we were to appreciate it. Family traditions, like gathering together for the evening meal, were things that definitely worked. Even to this day, with all of us being older and in different states, when we get together at the table during holidays or other occasions my mother always bursts into tears of happiness and nostalgia. We feel the same way.

Here's the thing about dessert. I always served dessert. Sometimes it was a couple of cookies or—on the weekends—something fancier. Maybe it was just an ice-cream cone, but it was always a dessert, no matter what. I think my kids liked the idea that at the end of a meal there was the promise of *something* delicious. Often, there was a nice bowl of fruit on the table. The kids would be more likely to pick up a piece of fruit if it was sitting there, rather than immediately going for some sweets.

Don't bribe your kids with dessert or another treat so they will try a new food or finish their meal. It will always be a tug-of-war if you do. Don't blame yourself, though, if your child is picky about certain foods. When Kenny was a little guy, he was so picky; no matter what I cooked, he'd look at me and say, "I want 'Tucky Fried Chicken." Even though Brian swears my fried chicken is still better than the Colonel's, it did not stop Kenny from asking for KFC. Julius would often say, "Go get my baby 'Tucky Fried Chicken."

Don't Be Too Busy to Be Together

Teenage years are often the height of busy activities. Andre played football and all the kids had some activities and work schedules, but that didn't have to disrupt our family time, especially our dinnertime. The thing is, just about the time teenagers get busy, they need to be part of the family more than ever. Tell your crew it's OK to say to a friend: "I can't stay any longer; I have to go home for dinner."

Anyway, in my opinion, there are way too many organized activities going on, especially for the youngest kids. I think it takes childhood away from them. Where is the spontaneity? Some families keep their kids so busy I wonder if it is because the parents just can't be bothered. Is it possible some parent thinks his company or a family dinner is not worth more than an art lesson? He needs to wise up because it isn't true.

Make Everyone Part of the Dinner Process

Our brownstone kitchen was unusually large. Julius had an island put in during a renovation, and this was our gathering place. The little Rocks gathered after school to do homework on one side while I prepared dinner on the other.

Each evening, by 6:30 P.M. the space was cleaned. Based on the chore chart assignments, the kids got busy. Chris would get the plates, Tony folded the napkins, and Brian put ice in the glasses and so on. Children take pride in the simplest things.

If you don't have a chore chart already, it's simple to make one up. Assign each of your children a chore to do for the family meal and put the chore next to their name on a paper list. Make sure everyone can see it.

Brian: One detail always stands out in my memories of our house. When my mother cooked, she would sing. We'd come into the kitchen sometimes just to hear her sing. She liked all kinds of music, including Barbra Streisand, Crystal Gayle, and Linda Ronstadt.

Ally: Each of us had a job to do. We learned about consequences. If you sat down and the Kool-Aid was warm, it meant somebody didn't put water in the ice tray or forgot to put in the ice.

Don't bore your kids to death by giving them the same chore every week. My kids traded everything—clothes, games, even the food on their plates, along with the chores. Nothing wrong with that; it teaches them to bargain.

A special chore for one lucky person was to go upstairs and wake Daddy for dinner (he worked nights). Everyone would wait to hear his footsteps coming down the stairs. It was the exciting part.

Don't Leave the Baby Behind

It is never too early to start. Pull up the high chair to the table and bring the baby in to so-cialize, even if it is only the three of you. Our babies were never excluded from the family circle. Many people have their kids eat at a little table and make a mess while the parents eat elsewhere. I don't understand it.

Sit the little guy down with breadsticks or crackers. When Chris was out of the pram, I bought the seat that hooked onto the side of the table. It was convenient. Anyway, keep a plate of food ready so if the baby is whining and the roast is in the oven, warm up the plate and you are all set.

There are always options and solutions. One definite *no-can-do* option is to tell a cranky or restless child: "Shut up, dinner will be ready in a minute." Kids don't understand why you are upset; a two-year-old only knows he wants to eat right now.

> **MAMA'S MOJO** Naturally, when you are making dinner, the baby always wants to eat. Solution: save leftovers to make a little plate. Keep it in the fridge, fresh and ready to warm up when you need it. During dinner, he can have dessert while the family is enjoying the meal.

Lay Down Table Rules Before You Sit Down

Every family should set out rules for the family meal. If you haven't had any rules, it will be tough at first. Some will still want to watch TV or eat elsewhere. Be sure to follow through; it will get easier with more and more to talk about each time. You might also want rules for servings and seconds. Our dinner table had these rules:

1. Only ask for what you plan to eat. Seconds? Thirds? Sure. You can get it, but you better eat it. We were not going to throw good food away, period.

2. No one could bring food into our household unless there was enough for everyone. This was a strictly enforced rule. If a child did not want to share, he better eat it away from our house.

We also wanted to instill in each child how they should take care of each other. After all, we wouldn't allow one child to chow down on a pizza slice in front of his family if no one else had any. Some of this sharing habit came from Julius. He would always tell the kids that if his family just had one "crumb" to eat—one "crumb"—he would break it up to share with his brothers and sisters. So, my kids had better forget about not sharing a pizza slice or a bag of fries.

Stop the Distractions

Chris and I have a bad breakfast habit: we will never sit down to eat without a newspaper or magazine—even in a restaurant. Maybe it's OK at breakfast (if that's not your main family meal), but don't read the paper at the dinner table.

As a matter of fact, shut off the TV before the evening meal. Turn off iPods and computers—lose the cell phones. Don't allow toys or games, either. Parents—as tempting as it is—don't bring the mail to the table. Make it an island of calm for your day. If you are not strict about it, many family-time benefits will be lost. In addition, kids eat better when their attention is not pulled in different directions.

Make Every Dinner Together an Occasion

You don't need to prepare a four-course dinner from scratch to have the benefits of a family meal. It doesn't matter what you serve. Even if it's fast food or takeout, you must have everyone sit down together at the table. We've eaten sub-sandwiches from the corner deli and had the best evening by just relaxing and sharing. It's important to eat in the same room together.

> MAMA'S MOJO Don't plan regular family meals that require intricate steps. Why be cranky with the kids because your soufflé flopped? What your kids want is you. Be there in mind and body as you sit down.

One of our best take-out times was fried fish night with our "catch" from Nostrand and Pacific in New York. It's gone now, but we remember it well. The lines to the place always ran around the block. Many a weekend I would go there and get a bucket of fish and bread with fries for the family. I'd also make a big pot of grits. The table would be set that night with paper plates and we'd have soda as a treat. We still talk about that crispy fish and how the conversations always flowed during those delicious evenings of minimal preparation.

Sometimes, in the early days of TV dinners, I bought each of the kids a tin-plate special. They thought it was the greatest thing. The hands-down favorite was the fried chicken TV dinner with that little dessert. (The funny thing was, we never watched TV while eating TV dinners.)

Like everyone else, we had times when things were tight in our household. We were a partnership, Julius and I, and we never wanted our children to ever worry about anything. Both Brian and Tony reminded me recently of the times when I served simple grilled cheese sandwiches and soup as if it were a special occasion. They remembered that the presentation was lovely with the sandwiches all arranged into quarters on the plate. The kids thought they were being rewarded with a fine supper. Later, when they were older, they figured out it was because money was tight and that's all we could serve at that moment. Brian laughed when told me he didn't stop to think until he was grown about the real meaning of "grilled cheese nights."

MAMA'S MOJO We had a game for drinks at the table: Full Cup/Half a Cup/Drop. The kids all got a **full cup** of a beverage when we began the meal, then a **half-cup** refill for seconds, and finally **just a drop** if they really wanted some more. We started that game so the kids wouldn't have too much liquid at night (you know what that can do). It's a great way of having fun and putting a stop to a potential problem.

Enjoy Family Meals Away from Home

Sometimes, the family table was not at home. When the kids were little, we went to Junior's restaurant in Brooklyn almost every weekend. When they got older, we would pick places around the city to visit together.

Later, when my boys were in Little League we'd drive many times on the Belt Parkway all the way out to Queens for a game. On those game nights, we'd eat at White Castle Hamburgers.

Be sure to review home dinner rules with your young kids before you eat out. Share what isn't acceptable (like running all over the restaurant or loud talk). Bring along books or crayons for the littlest ones to keep them busy. Talk about this special family time away from your house. It's wise to pack a little tray of snacks like carrot sticks for your youngest to munch on while waiting for the meal.

Set the Table for Talk

Once the kids get a full stomach, things loosen up. They not only eat the beans—they spill the beans. Everything would come out at the table, especially secrets. The higher the comfort level, the more talk came out—especially news about what the other kids were doing. It all happened right at the dinner table. Everybody knew whatever came out could be laughed off (most things anyway) and no one would get "killed."

Teach your children at an early age to talk around the table.

Kids learn new words and how to ask questions or tell a story when they are involved in a conversation like that. Get it across to kids that there is nothing they cannot talk about within the confines of your home. A child must know he can always come home and tell the worst (if he has to) and the family is there to help. Many times a big problem is made smaller when brothers and sisters join in to support and make it less of a burden.

Even the good-natured bantering and put-downs between family members serve a good purpose. Our crew learned to have a thick skin—a great survival skill for grown-up life.

> **MAMA'S MOJO** Parents, don't use the dinner table
> to moan about work or complain about disappointments in
> your life. Stop the kids from fighting with each other and
> don't bring up something that ticked you off last week.
> This is the time to share and to learn more
> about your children.

Dinner Is a Fact-Finding Mission

At dinner, we talked about whatever happened in the neighborhood and the world, and we made it funny. When we lived in Bedford-Stuyvesant it could be rough, but we always found the humor in it. We talked about what was on TV and we got around to smoking, drinking, and other kids' problems. There were so many teachable moments during dinner. In the most relaxed and secure way, we could explore possibilities, morals, behavior, and family cultural attitudes in between the soup and dessert. What a mouthful!

Parents, realize that dinner is a fact-finding mission. Get your information through the laughter; listen to what is going on and what is not being said. You have to learn to cue into each child so you understand what is really happening. For instance, one child might get loud when he is upset or quiet when he is content. Another child gets noisy when he is happy—it is important to figure this out. Keep in mind, though, the one who talks on Monday may have nothing to say on Tuesday. Try to listen to what a child actually says by watching body language, tone of voice, and eye contact as much as what is coming out of his mouth.

Kids get frustrated if they feel a parent can't understand them. It makes them miserable and crazy. When you establish a regular connection point—like a family meal—it creates the opportunity to exchange information with your children so you can understand each other better.

How can you know who your children are if you don't know what they think, what they do at school or work, or what bothers them? A daily chance to catch up is critical for finding out about what's up. Don't be too busy to listen carefully, or you will be much busier trying to make things right with your kids down the road.

Start with what went on at school. We also loved to talk about what was going to happen on the weekend, and lots of good gossip about family and friends. If someone talked about future party plans, we got a heads-up about it. Listen closely, you'll hear the name of the friend who is having the party, where it is being held, and what other friends might come along. You can also get a sense of what's what from the responses around the table to the party plans.

Julius and I talked about our work and shared some insights and some not-so-pleasant things, too. We always let our children know the truth, because whatever we had to face, they may have to face someday—like racism on the job.

We always had so much to share. As the boys grew up and had outside jobs, our dinner crowd grew smaller, but the boys didn't miss out. When they came home, whatever the time, at least one parent would always sit with them while they ate, to catch up on what was happening in their lives.

Travel the World from Your Table

We also learned about life from those who joined our family at the dinner table. I guess our house was like a melting pot; we always had friends over from everywhere, including people from work. It was fun for the kids to see our friend Jerry, who is Jewish, ask for seconds of my Southern cooking.

> **MAMA'S MOJO** It's best to let your kids know that all people are just people—what better way than by having many different types of people join you for a meal around the family table. We have entertained every race, culture, religion, nationality, and economic group I can think of. It has helped my children understand something about the people of the world they live in. That will always help them.

We encouraged the children to bring their friends home. The kids incorporated their friends into our family dinner. That way, we always knew who their friends were. Bringing friends into the family life adds a level of respect. It also was an eye-opener for some. One child who was a guest at dinner told us he thought only "people on TV" sat down and had dinner. He learned at our house that real people do this and how good it is.

> MAMA'S MOJO When you invite your children's friends home, you get the chance to see them in *action*. It's a great time—after they've loosened up a bit—to ask questions about their attitudes and encourage them to join the discussion along with everyone else. If a friend behaves badly at the table, you don't have to say a thing. If they do well, you have cemented respect for your child and your family from his friend—that's a good thing.

Sometimes, my children learned about worlds they could not have imagined unless they saw it for themselves. For example, one day there was a new sister at the table. My children were introduced to this foster child as her new family. After dinner was over, she got up from the table and literally went over to the kitchen garbage can and started eating out of it. The boys started to giggle. I explained to them why she didn't understand she could eat as much as she wanted at our house. Before coming to us, I told them, she had to scrounge in the garbage to survive. It opened their eyes to the world outside our home's warmth and security.

This was true of many foster children who couldn't adjust easily to the bountiful food available in our house. One girl's story was particularly moving. She'd often gone days without food. The refrigerator in her house had a lock and key. Finally, she was so hungry she took a twenty-dollar bill from a hiding place she'd discovered and ran away to a fast-food restaurant. She indulged all day and kept on eating until closing time. She was taken into foster care and one day ended up with us at our dinner table.

You CAN Send Your Biscuits to Hollywood

Food from the family table is often a revered memory. Some favorites stand out in your mind; the smell of them takes you home. Chris always asked me to send biscuits when he first left home. I'd bake up a fresh batch, cover them in foil, and have FedEx come pick them up at my house. I can only imagine the Hollywood types who saw him open his FedEx package and pull out some fine Southern biscuits.

Randy Richardson: Mama Rock was a great cook. Her chicken and rice was my favorite. Their dinner table was a good influence, and I do that now with my children. But, LORD, her biscuits were it—they really were it!

I also baked pies for my kids and mailed them. It is still a big hit. The kids say not only was the pie good, but when they warmed it in the oven their place smelled like our house.

Food is sacred that way; it is part of our own family culture. Every family has that favorite dish or baked good to bring back all those happy days at home.

C'mon Inside the Rock Family Kitchen—Tips & Recipes

I learned to cook from my mother-in-law, Mary Rock. She was the mother of fourteen children. All her life she cooked these huge pots of food—I didn't even know they made pots that size. She'd make delicious stews and fabulous chicken with scallions. Even after her children moved on, she'd still cook these big meals. Often, she'd invite half the neighborhood and, of course, all her grown-up children who could make it back home for the evening. Sometimes, even before Julius and I got married, we fell into the habit of getting into our cars after work and finding ourselves on Koskiosko Street at his mama's house ready to polish off a dinner.

Aside from Mary Rock's lessons, I had to figure out the rest of the cooking business; I never learned as a child because my mother always made the meals. Julius was my guinea pig for my early meal creations. You know, that man never let on that he didn't like my cooking at the start. One time I overheard him say, "Boy, Rose could not cook worth a damn in the beginning, but I'd never hurt her feelings." I guess he ate all my experiments and never said a word. What a man! Later, of course, when I finally got the hang of it, my kids and Julius would outdo each other with genuine compliments over what I learned to make. (By the way, I never let on about hearing Julius's remark, and he never told me about it.)

Andre: We used to have contests among the family over who could give my mother most or best compliments. Another great thing about her—she would try to make whatever you liked; she paid close attention to what all of us kids wanted and tried to prepare it to please everyone at least some of the time.

My children had individual likes, dislikes, and favorites. There was a fan for each type of chicken: baked, fried, or chicken and rice. Even the most demanding eater (like Kenny) might try something new if you use sneaky tricks. Slip in some sliced squash next to a slice of pizza. Some kids will try anything if it is next to a favorite food or even mixed in it. Don't make a big deal out of it—try again later if it doesn't work. Most kids don't take to a new food right away; it is often an acquired taste. As kids grow up, they are more flexible. That still doesn't mean they will like everything. Some people never learn to like broccoli, for instance, but everyone loved my smothered chicken and biscuits.

Original Smothered Chicken and Biscuits

All these recipes are pure country, comfort foods. Old-fashioned Southern cooks never measured. It was done in dips and dabs, a pinch of this and a little of that. This recipe was done for the opening of "Comedy Nation in New York City,"

*but it has been my family's favorite for years. Oh yes, long
ago it was made with fat renderings. Today, I make it with
extra virgin olive oil.*

You will need:
chicken fryer parts
flour
celery, onion, scallions
extra virgin olive oil
garlic pepper, seasoning salt

Heat oil in skillet (don't forget olive oil burns easily). Season
chicken to taste, lightly flour. Brown chicken on each side
and remove from skillet. Chop celery, onions, and scallions.
Add to skillet and sauté until tender. Return chicken to pan,
add ½ cup water, cover, and cook approximately 25 minutes
or until tender.

Biscuits

You will need:
flour (self-rising)
2% milk
Crisco shortening

In a bowl, cut shortening into the flour until there is no loose
flour. Add milk to bowl and stir just enough to mix together.
On a floured surface and with floured hands, knead dough
until it is not sticky and can be easily rolled and cut into
biscuits. Bake at 350 degrees from 12 to 15 minutes until
golden brown.

No Frills Never Meant No Fun

Randy Richardson, who is just like family, still likes to call me a "no frills" mama. I'm also a "no name" mama when I buy "no name" brands because I'm naturally thrifty, or, as some would say, cheap. I actually tried peanut butter and jelly packaged together in the same container, too. Chris told me that's like buying a shoe with the sock already in it. I think the big idea is to keep your budget as your bottom line and get creative in the kitchen.

Sometimes, the most inexpensive ingredients turn into recipes that are your family favorites. One of those is my "Beans and Franks" special.

Tony: I'm a wings guy, so my mama always gave me the wings on any chicken, baked or fried. She also made great wingettes! I'm a simple guy, so my all-time favorite is her "Beans and Franks" special. Understand now, ethnic black people's beans and franks are different than regular hot dogs and beans. For one thing, they are served with a pot of white rice alongside. It is all sooo good.

Jordan: I drew a picture and wrote a poem on a card for my mom glorifying the "smells of her kitchen." It still smells good in there. I love her "Beans and Franks" special. When I wrote the card, I was thinking about that dish.

MAMA'S MOJO WING TIP

Before wingettes ever came out commercially, I'd take a chicken wing, cut off the tip, and cut it in half. I used to cook dozens of them. The twins from the neighborhood—Troy and Roy—used to joke about them as "pigeon wings" because they were so small. They still make great snacks and party tidbits for a reasonable price.

"ROCK-STYLE" Beans and Franks

You will need:
all beef or turkey smoked sausage
1 large can of vegetarian baked beans
extra virgin olive oil
spicy mustard (optional)
black pepper
onion
barbeque sauce
catsup

Heat oil in heavy skillet, slice sausage, dice onions. Add sausage and onion to oil and sauté until onions are cooked. Add vegetarian baked beans and stir. Add barbeque sauce and catsup to taste. Bring to simmer. Dust with black pepper. Serve over hot white rice.

The Pie Secret Revealed: A Crusty Tip

Although we are not sitting at my table, I'm going to let a secret slip right now. When people would ask why my pies were so darn good, I'd just smile. I never told them, but I'm going to give you a tip. It's only two words: orange juice. Yes, I'd add a little orange juice to the pie. It makes it tart and delicious. Try it when you make the sweet potato pie recipe; you will be impressed.

Mama Rock's Sweet Potato Pie

Pie shell: Try a frozen pie shell or Pillsbury ready-to-roll-out crust.
You will need:

2–3 large sweet potatoes
2 large eggs
1/2 cup granulated sugar
1/2 cup brown sugar
1/4 cup evaporated milk
1/2 cup orange juice with pulp
1 cup evaporated milk
1 stick of butter
1 tsp cinnamon
1 tsp nutmeg
1 1/2 tsp vanilla

Peel and boil the sweet potatoes until tender. Mash or puree in a blender. Set aside. Melt the stick of butter. Set aside. In a bowl, mix until smooth the eggs, sugars, and evaporated milk. Then, mix together with the sweet potato puree. Add the melted butter, orange juice, vanilla, cinnamon, and nutmeg. Mix together until smooth. Pour into prepared pie shell. Bake at 350 degrees for 20–25 minutes. Let cool.

It's Never Too Late to Call the Family for Dinner

Even if you just now decided family meals are a good idea—it's not too late. As long as someone is still home, mealtime is all about sharing. The value of it will be evident because (I promise) it is going to open new lines of communication. With all the crazy schedules and kids coming and going, your family meal can provide an anchor. Teens need it as much as your youngest child. So, start tonight. It may seem a bit awkward at first, but soon, you'll wonder how you ever got along without it.

Remember Mama Rock's Rules and Strategies

■ Feed Them and They Will Tell You Everything

Much is learned at the dinner table. It's the heart and soul of a family—and the best place to snoop out what's really going on with your kids.

■ Make Everyone Part of the Dinner Process

Don't exclude anyone—even the baby—from your table. Assign dinner prep chores to instill pride and a sense of being part of a family event.

■ Stop the Distractions Before You Sit Down

Before you gather for the family meal, lose the cell phones and TV. Make that time an island of calm for your day—the kids will eat better, too.

■ Make Every Meal an Occasion

It's not about the food—even takeout works—it's about the opportunity to eat and share together with your kids every day.

- **Dinner Is a Fact-Finding Mission**

  Kids not only eat beans, they spill them. Make the family table a comfortable place to share what's really going on (no matter what).

- **Travel the World from Your Table**

  The best way to learn about life is to interact with people from different cultures, races, nationalities, and religions. Invite them to your family table.

- **You CAN Send Your Biscuits to Hollywood**

  Food from the family table is often a revered memory. Mail some favorites—the familiar aroma and taste is a temporary homesickness cure.

- **It's Never Too Late to Call the Family for Dinner**

  Family mealtime is an anchor; it's never too late to start. Your whole family will wonder how you lived without it (dinner that is, not my recipe for Smothered Chicken and Biscuits).

5

You Are Whatever You Answer To

Gotta be true, to what ya do and keep
ya game up.

—Tupac Shakur

LOOK, IT'S A COMPLICATED WORLD out there for our kids—between peer pressure and media influences like TV and the movies, no wonder they get confused. A goal for parents is to help our children believe in themselves and their unlimited potential. That's the most important game to keep up for our kids. Help them get the point by your good examples of positive actions and reactions. And, help them not to think or talk badly about themselves.

Respect the Need for R.E.S.P.E.C.T.

Despite my humiliating experience at Rosemary School when I was left behind during a special Thanksgiving lunch, I was fortunate to attend that school, after all. Why? Because of someone named Mr. Joseph Thompson, the principal. He was a fine man who instituted rules that gave us a sense of worth. For instance, he required certain conduct from his students: boys had to wear ties, and girls wore dresses instead of pants. The school was kept in excellent condition. All across South Carolina, he set a superior standard. Because he was a stickler for instilling self-respect and personal pride, he helped us all.

I learned from him not to answer to someone who had low expectations or unfounded negative feelings toward me. I also learned not to accept what someone did or said if it made me feel bad. He taught us not to stand there and take it. His advice? If people say negative things about you—*prove them wrong*. It really inspired me. I'm honored to pass that advice along to you.

Don't Quack Like a (Gangsta) Duck— Unless You Are a (Gangsta) Duck!

In the long run, if children aren't taught independence, they lack self-confidence—that creates the worst kind of problems. The thing is, if they are not taught to be individuals, they will not be self-confident. When that happens, your children are liable to believe or become whatever anybody or anything says about them. After all, how can they figure out who they are?

If your daughter hangs out in trashy clothes and acts cheap, how can she be surprised if a guy says something low-down to her? Maybe she's one of those young women who dresses provocatively but is secretly scared to show her body. Her girlfriends do it, so she does it too.

Remember the old saying: *If it walks like a duck and quacks like a duck—it might be a duck.* Tell your girls: if they dress and act like a "ho," they just might be thought to be one. If nothing else, they could be a victim of "duck-profiling."

Now *Gangstas*—that's another story. *Gangsta wannabees* wear clothes that are about to slip off, and they love to act the fool—especially when they spout *Ebonics*, a supposed black language. Language? Listen up—there is no honest black language like that. If your child uses *Ebonics*, it means he doesn't care enough to speak correctly. Urban black kids in the projects aren't the only ones who emulate this kind of subculture—one that encourages kids to act uneducated in order to be "cool." White kids, suburban blacks, and others proudly rush to answer to this loser label. After a while, it's not playacting or dressing up anymore. Kids can become what they answer to: genuine losers.

You Are Who You Are With

One thing is still the same: parents who care are selective about who their children hang out with. Parents, do you know your kids' friends? If you don't, it's time right now to find out fast. Help your brood take a realistic look at who they are "hanging with." Explain how some things never change; every person is judged by the company he keeps. Old people would say (when I was a kid): *If you lay down with dogs, you get up with fleas.* When your child associates with "someone" or a group of "someones," he will start taking on their characteristics or habits sooner or later (quack-quack).

What can you do as a parent? Of course, you can't pick out your children's friends for them. But you can encourage them to go to places where they can meet "worthwhile friends." If they still end up with the wrong "crew," you have to make a judgment call, even if it isn't popular.

For one thing, start to redirect your child away from badly chosen friends—just like you did with other harmful choices when he was a toddler. You may end up going to the movies with your child, but that's better than having him or her go out with the wrong crowd. Find things to do on weekends so your child doesn't have time for those people.

The Need to Belong Is Sometimes Wrong

Sometimes, I think the need to belong can stunt a kid's growth. Being a part of a group means your child will give up some or all of his individuality just to fit in. It's different than peer pressure—it's about the strong need to belong—even if it's wrong. Maybe your child wants to be in this or that group but doesn't have enough of what it takes (good or bad). He might try to belong to that crowd anyway out of the fear of being labeled a nerd or worry that he'll be left on the sidelines. For example, some girls will hang out with certain kids even if they don't LIKE them or enjoy the places they go or their parties, just so they can "fit in" with a "desirable" clique. In the end, kids usually feel lonely when they are in the wrong crowd and not doing what they feel comfortable with or want to do.

Step up to tell a child it's OK to be a majority of one. Say it repeatedly in different ways. Show a child it is "cool" just to be himself. Luckily, most kids find what their parents say more important in determining their self-esteem than their peer group (believe it or not). Hey, parents, you have the responsibility and the advantage as long as you step up to take it.

Bust the Media's Myth

Young girls are bombarded by music videos and movies featuring women with seriously sexy clothes. Whether they understand it or not, young people want to be part of the glamorous world they see paraded in front of their faces.

Parents, why complain about your twelve-year-old who dresses like a tart and grumble about how bad your boy looks in his huge, oversized clothes? They may have seen those styles on BET or MTV, but children don't buy their clothes—you do! And, where were you when they got ready to go out? Your responsibility lies in seeing if they are *properly* dressed.

So, stop it before it happens. And explain the truth about the media. Explain why sex sells, how advertising creates "wants" and conveys unreal lifestyles as normal. It may be old hat to parents, but it's news to kids, who are the biggest target and are the most gullible. Listen, there are new hip-hop marketing companies whose whole reason for existence is to focus on the teenage market. So, you can just imagine.

While you are at it, don't forget to reveal the secret of how the airbrush, paint, makeup, and other strategic techniques work together to make those "perfect" photographs of models and stars in magazines and tabloids and ever-present music videos. You need to bring it out in the open and discuss these issues. Put the media back where they belong (trying to sell something, mostly to your kids).

Help your boys and girls look at real women and men around them. Help your daughters stop comparing themselves to these idealized "media women." Discuss how they don't need to compare to the small percentage of models or movie, TV, and MTV stars who set these "standards." This is important; teenagers need to believe they don't have to be anyone other than the best version of who they already are. It can help with any urges they get to blindly dress like a tramp, develop eating disorders, or do or say things they don't believe in solely to fit in to some media ideal. They don't have to answer to that.

Quit Talking Bad About Yourself

If someone called me a bitch to my face, I'd want to slap him. Nobody can call me a bitch. If your daughter turns around and answers someone who calls her a bitch (or worse) pray that she has a perception problem. If your son does the same when someone yells a racial epithet or ethnic slur, it's time to question what he thinks about himself. If a guy yells out in a busy area, "Hey, stupid," look to see who turns around. If someone does, I hope it is not your child.

The word "nigger" has an awful meaning when used by a white person. The "n" word never caused me much discomfort because I knew what a nigger was. Since I knew I wasn't one, *why would I answer* or react to it? After all, we only become what someone calls or labels us IF we answer to it and accept it. Your kids need to understand that.

As you teach your children not to answer to anyone else's "putdowns" or unrealistic media expectations, make sure your kids don't put themselves down either. I have always taught Andi to put a high value on herself. Unless she believes it, what her brothers and I say won't be enough.

Tell your girls, when a guy says, "you are so pretty," they should answer (or at least think it), "I know, thank you." That way, she is already ahead of the game and won't blindly follow the first man who gives her a compliment. After all, that won't be the first time she heard it.

Of course, beauty is not the only attribute of an adolescent. Compliment other qualities like talents, kindness, and good grades or sports abilities.

The heart of the matter is this: if your child values himself, because you have helped him understand who he is and instilled confidence through your upbringing, he will answer to his own authority. Wouldn't it be great if every child had parents, grandparents, or other adults in his life who loved, honored, and respected him? It would let a child know he mattered. Be that person for your children and anyone who needs it—we gotta "backtalk the badtalk" children say about themselves!

Catch Your Kid Doing Something Good

Establishing a routine and rules—like I said before—is critical because of the security and self-confidence it creates in children. That is the greatest thing in raising kids; to instill in them a sense of self-reliance: the ability to do well when they are not with you—so they can make the right choices.

> **MAMA'S MOJO** Being self-reliant includes the ability to learn from what went wrong. Figure out together what might have been better—and come to a positive conclusion. Don't ever forget to **show your kids what they did right every chance you get.** Emphasize positive intentions—and praise, praise, praise whenever you can.

Keep in mind all the rules, regulations, and ideas your child has learned up to this point. If you have set the stage with rules, responsibilities, and consequences for your children, they will learn self-esteem and their self-reliance will grow. One thing does not change: those kids with self-worth have more self-control over the choices offered to them.

Brian: When I was at Benedict College, people I met kept asking me: "Are you going Greek? What fraternity are you pledging?" One guy even asked me how I could possibly define myself if I'm not a member of a fraternity. I answered him this way: "Before I join your frat, I'll start my own." My mother has repeated this story many times. She always adds, "How did I raise such a self-confident person?" She sure did. I think it was praise and love more than anything.

Don't Bow to the Power of the Peers

Jordan loves soccer. He's played the game since he was four years old. He's good at it. Last year, at the first meeting of the new players, he was assigned to a team. He was the only black kid on the team—Jordan has often been the only black kid on a team. Some of his black friends asked why he played soccer because no black

Tony: We were independent as kids. I didn't drink until I was maybe twenty-five years old. I had friends who were drinking in junior high. My friends knew it was not *my thing. It was cool because I was cool about it. I never smoked a cigarette. I never smoked weed. Comics drink and smoke a lot of the time. I think it's more important to get high off other things, to feel comfortable in your own skin, and not to try to be the next person.*

kids played the game in our area. They implied it was a game for white kids. He let himself be led by his peers because he didn't want his friends to think he was "trying to be white." He still loves the game, but he was not true to himself because he no longer plays on the team.

If your child likes to read, does he feel he must hide his books because some friends might think reading is a waste of time? A friend of mine told me she knew her son did his homework every night, because she checked it. During a school conference she discovered he rarely turned it in. When she confronted him, he told her it wasn't cool to do too well. His friends thought that all guys—especially black guys—shouldn't be too smart. Are they serious?

{ **MAMA'S MOJO** Find out what kind of advice your child's peers give him. Ask your child casually about what his buddies think on a certain subject. No matter what he tells you, don't "diss" that friend, ever. Simply suggest another alternative—after all, kids are easily swayed. If that doesn't work, use the classic: "If your friend jumped off a bridge, would you do it too?" That old thing still works—it does; if nothing else, it makes your kid think before jumping into anything! }

Don't Throw in the Towel—Snap It!

Maybe your child doesn't bow to peer pressure—he just bows out because of it. Although Jordan bowed out of soccer because of his peers, some kids quit music, sports, or other important activities because they are afraid of being embarrassed in front of their friends if they goof up or aren't at the top right away.

> MAMA'S MOJO Speak up. Talk about the times you or other family members made a mistake in front of your peers—and did just fine anyway, thank you. Address those fears if you suspect your child might harbor them. No peer pressure should make your child quit something that can help him or could make his life richer. Chances are, he probably loved what he was doing—so help support that.

Take a Bite of BBQ from a Silver Spoon

Parents, as you teach your child to have the courage of his convictions, help him with the smaller things too. For example, maybe he really likes BBQ but doesn't want to eat it in front of some of his "elite" friends because it's such a *black* thing. It seems like no big deal, but it is a compromise of who he is. Small compromises always lead to bigger ones.

Some black people hear blues—the genuine, old-fashioned

kind—and say, "Oh, that's so ghetto." Even though they love that music, they'll say something else instead—"I really like Barry Manilow"—because it is more acceptable to them. These are people who are ashamed of who they are—they stereotype themselves!

Teach your children how every culture is multifaceted. Show them why it is possible to like old-fashioned blues and still love the opera or like country and classical music equally. I love the blues but had season tickets to the opera. Some of my friends don't understand why I like it, but they have not bothered to come along to give it a try. I'd never miss the opera just because my friends don't appreciate it. Likewise, your child should never miss something he wants to do because his friends don't appreciate it or because they make fun of it.

If They Don't Accept You Because of Your Hair: Don't Be There

Mervin "Spectac" Jenkins, Brian's college friend, was worried about his dreadlocks when he applied for a school administrator position. The school he applied to expressed an interest but told him to cut his hair. He asked my advice. I said: "If people won't accept you because of your hair, you don't want to be there." He went on to become an assistant principal of that school and continued with his music as a rap artist. If you are honestly OK with yourself and someone has a problem with it, the problem is usually with the other person.

Go ahead, lick the BBQ sauce from your fingers. Maybe another time, have caviar on a silver fork. Live a full life and show your kids how it's done. Otherwise, you demonstrate to your children how to deny the essence of who they are and what they enjoy.

A certain group doesn't have to be solely identified with a particular kind of music, theater, food, or hairstyle. Tell your kids this: when they get tired of that empty feeling of fooling themselves if they do what they don't truly want to do, you will be there to remind them about another way. After all, there's a whole world to explore.

Remember Where You Came From

When I am asked to speak in public, I often talk about the way I was brought up. I mention what I did back then, like clean houses or pick cotton. Who do I help if I don't tell the truth or if I deny where I come from, especially if those who listen only see me as I am today: an educator, parent, and active community member despite—or even because of—those hard times.

I know plenty of people who don't want anyone to know they didn't have a bathroom when they were growing up. Hey, most blacks in the South didn't have an indoor bathroom. Many others in this country didn't have one either. My sense is, it would "kill" some of those people who have reinvented themselves if word got out how they grew up poor—or actually picked cotton in the day. Now you tell me, 90 percent of the blacks growing up in the South picked cotton—if "nobody" was involved, how did it get picked?

The thing with me is this: I'm proud of where I came from. That's why I appreciate where I am now. If I didn't think back to the days when I was someone's housekeeper, I don't think I would appreciate my housekeeper the way I do. Maybe that's why I treat her like a person instead of a fixture—the way I was treated.

> **MAMA'S MOJO** Give your son or daughter a journal; it is a powerful tool for self-discovery. It doesn't have to be fancy—even dollar stores carry them (I ought to know). Just encourage them to jot down thoughts, feelings, dreams, and observations of the world around them. Don't read it, parents; I know it's hard not to. It will be of great value to them now and in the future to remember the way it was—and share it with their children.

By learning about the "way it was," kids can see the big picture. They can learn to appreciate the basic values of hard work, discipline, and the sacrifices of people who went before them. They can learn about who they "are" and where they came from. However, as black parents we can't wait around for the schools to teach our children about their background. We have to let our kids know our black history is not something to be taught one month a year beginning on February 1. (Who relegated our history to once a year—and the shortest month at that?) We need to teach our kids about their people all year long. If our kids don't know the struggle, they don't know the legacy of a rich heritage. If they don't know who they are, they end up looking to find it out

Quick crib notes: The Little Rock Nine were a group of black high school students in Little Rock, Arkansas. They went down in history books together when President Dwight Eisenhower had to intervene after Arkansas governor Orval Faubus tried to prevent the students from entering the segregated Central High School in 1957. Each one of the "Nine" went on to become successful—one was a member of President Jimmy Carter's cabinet.

through—you guessed it—the media and all that garbage they see on TV. Then they think: "Hey, this is us, right?"

Julius and I let our kids know what a great heritage they had inherited. We read James Baldwin, went to off-Broadway plays by August Wilson—anything we could. We learned about black history in our house. We covered the distant and the recent past. Hey, too many black kids don't even know what the Civil Rights movement was all about. If you grabbed some black kids off the street and asked them about the Little Rock Nine, they'd probably think you were talking about a new rock group. Forget about them being able to recognize Stokely Carmichael's name or the Southern Christian Leadership Council—you get the picture.

Why not teach your children about brave, bright, self-reliant, and courageous people from your *own* ethnic, religious, or cultural background? Let them understand and identify with them. All children, especially black children, can learn from the story of little Ruby Bridges.

Help your children learn to answer to their own authority—not what others label them—and to the greater authority of what is right in this world. Teach them to be self-reliant by reinforcing the value of being true to one's self—of having the courage of their own convictions.

Six-year-old Ruby's courage in 1960, the year desegregation became a law, is still a breathtaking inspiration. She walked into the William Frantz School in New Orleans, Louisiana, on the first day under the new law to integrate the classrooms. Accompanied by U.S. Marshals, she walked through a mean, jeering mob all the way to her first-grade class where she was the only pupil (no white students would join her). She was in the first grade—can you imagine that? Even so, Ruby never answered to the epithets the angry mob called her.

Ruby Bridges and her family answered the call to courage and a place in history. Most of us are not called upon for such difficult acts of bravery. Our children, however, need to learn about such strength.

Remember Mama Rock's Rules and Strategies

- Don't Quack Like a (Gangsta) Duck—Unless You Are a (Gangsta) Duck

  If your child dresses or acts like something he is not—and answers to it—tell him to be prepared to face the consequences.

- Bust the Media's Myth

  Expose your kids to the secrets and power of the media and why they don't have to answer to it.

- Quit Talking Bad About Yourself

  Teach your kids not to put themselves down—or believe other people when they hurl the "put-downs" at them.

- Catch Your Kid Doing Something Good

  Find ways to compliment your children if they do something right—it will create self-confidence and self-reliance.

- Don't Bow to the Power of the Peers

  Provide hints on how to make your child stop to think for a moment before blindly following his friends in whatever they say or do.

- Respect the Need for R.E.S.P.E.C.T.

  The importance of instilling self-respect can't be overlooked when it comes to raising successful children.

- Take a Bite of BBQ from a Silver Spoon

  Teach your children how every culture is multifaceted. Show them the importance of living a full life and not denying their essence.

- If They Don't Accept You Because of Your Hair: Don't Be There

  If your child can't be accepted somewhere for who she genuinely is, she shouldn't be in that situation or environment.

- Don't Hide the Way It Was

  Parents, talk about the good and the bad of where you came from—all of it. Don't hide your own upbringing or neglect teaching what made your people who they are today.

6

Reading Is Righteous

ONE OF THE LATE RAP artist Tupac Shakur's songs featured lyrics about Machiavelli. Jordan wanted to find out more. Can you imagine? This guy, who most people thought was a thug, got my son interested in a classic from the fifteenth century. Jordan was twelve years old when he asked me to buy the book *Prince and Principalities* by Niccolò Machiavelli. Tupac was a big reader too, and perhaps much deeper than most people imagined. He read everything.

Listen, I don't care what motivates a child to read—I just want to see it happen because I know what reading can do. I know the positive and important things it did for my children and what it can do for yours. If your child can read well, he will do better in school. Reading always equals doing better in everything because a reader can understand more and has a broader perspective.

Jordan reminded me of how magnificent it is simply to have the ability to read. When the Harry Potter series first came out, he'd stay up all night to read a new edition. Although I'd fuss and act like I didn't want to wait in line for a new "hot-off-the-press Harry," secretly I was happy. Jordan was in love with reading!

He came downstairs one morning and told me, "I need to thank Mrs. Walker." I asked him why he wanted to thank his former schoolteacher from years back. He looked at me and said, "Because she's the one who taught me to read."

Pass On a Reverence for Reading

I think my grandmother taught me to read early because she lived in an era when blacks were not encouraged to read—some were not allowed to read or were terribly punished for doing so. My great-grandfather was actually the one who took care of the slave owner's children. That's where he learned to read, and he taught my grandmother. She held a deep reverence for the importance of reading and passed it down to me.

With her excellent reading and writing skills, she took care of the paperwork for other black people. They'd bring their letters or other official things to her and she would help them. Even though she was not formally educated, she had such wisdom. She knew reading could take you places and expand you into a bigger world.

Because of this, I have such deep sadness when I see people of color who don't read. The mere fact that blacks were once denied the right to read or be educated makes me want every black person on this planet to walk around with a book and be an excellent reader. I think those who have been denied in the past should be on the forefront, fighting for the best education for their children and all minority children.

I started to read when I was around four years old. My brother James was three years older than me. He would be doing homework and my mother would help him; so my grandmother got out a book and taught me to read. By the time I was six or seven, I could read anything. I just had a "thing" for reading; I even read the announcements in church.

Randy Richardson: There were lots of books on black history at the Rock house. We had to be up on our black history and know who was who—we learned that from Mama Rock. She exposed us to things we were not getting in school.

Let Reading Feed Their Imagination

Your child's imagination can take him anywhere in this world. Reading helps create imagination as well. Both lead to learning and success both as a child and as an adult. Although I applaud the advances in technology that make information more available, in other ways I think introducing TV too freely to our kids is not a good thing. Many of us let them sit there in front of the tube with little or no interaction. There is no physical action and not much mental action either. An opportunity for children to visualize and develop their imagination is lost in front of the tube.

Looking back to my day—most parents said to shut off that "darn" TV. They did it because they didn't want to have a high power bill. A parent's favorite statement—*What do you think? I own the electric company?*—might have saved many of us from plopping in front of the TV all day watching cartoons.

Read to Keep Up with the World

My grandmother instilled in me how important it is to read a newspaper. Way back then, a paper was two cents a day. A dime could have meant food on the table—it didn't matter—she thought a newspaper was a requirement. I still read three or four newspapers daily. One of the things Chris and I share is our love of the written word—he's a newspaper nut like me.

My whole magazine "thing" started with the magazines my mother brought home from the women she cleaned for. Instead of throwing them out, they would give them to my mother. We would pore over each one. I think that's why I love magazines today. You name it, I subscribe to it.

Kenny: I see the importance of reading. It's my best hobby. I like history and nonfiction the most. Like my mother and Chrissy, I always read the newspaper. My mother stressed the need to read. She would read to me—to all of us. When I was in high school, I was the first one to get up and read aloud in front of the class. Other people were scared—not me. We had done that already, at home.

I know many people read the newspaper online these days. That's fine, especially at the office or on a commute with a laptop computer. The only problem is this: your children need to see you reading the paper. If they see you at the computer, you could be doing anything at all—not necessarily reading the news. Seeing the newspaper around the house might also encourage them to pick it up and read it—it's a good start to a lifelong love of the paper.

When Julius and I had first moved into Decatur Street, my parents came for a visit. I had left my newspapers and magazines piled high on top of a table. "See," my mother said to my father as she pointed to the big stack of my reading materials, "I told you that's why she knows everything—she reads everything." Lord, my parents thought no one was smarter than me. Even my brother John liked to hear me talk about books with my friends. He'd sit back and say proudly, "That's my sister."

Magazines are a wonderful way to get even reluctant readers to read. There are magazines for every interest—cars, fashion, model airplanes, sewing; whatever interests your child up through the teenage years can be found in a magazine that will keep him reading. It's fun to go through the magazines with your kids, too.

I honestly think I read everything because I saw others who did that same thing around me. That's something to keep in mind—how important it is to be a reading role model. For instance, although my Grandfather McClam was an African Methodist Episcopal (AME) Minister, he and my grandmother weren't the kind who pushed the Bible at us or insisted it was the only book worth reading. Instead, we were encouraged to read all kinds of books. My grandmother loved to read all kinds of things. Later in her life she even read *True Story*, an early romance magazine. Grandma McClam was something—she saw every facet of the world through reading and showed us how to do it too!

Read to Travel the World and Never Be Bored

When I was a girl, it was second nature to pick up a book (and talk about it). Other little girls and I could talk forever about a book like *The Secret of the Old Clock* in the Nancy Drew mystery series. We were never bored as we read about the *Bobbsey Twins* adventures (those books featured two sets of twins as lead characters). I guess Nancy Drew and the Bobbsey Twins were our Harry Potter—minus the special effects. Think back to your favorite childhood books and ask yourself what's best to share with your children or grandchildren.

If you consider it for a moment, you will realize that children have the opportunity to learn about children all over the world as they read. After all, I learned about the northeastern part of the country through the Bobbsey Twins. I searched for clues along the roads near Chicago with teenage detective Nancy Drew in her blue roadster. It kept me interested.

My school librarian introduced me to my all-time favorite book, *Little House in the Big Woods*, by Laura Ingalls Wilder. I checked that book out more than anybody in the history of Rosemary

School. I loved meeting all the prairie children. It was beautiful to imagine a family like theirs. I even enjoyed the TV series, *Little House on the Prairie*, based on those stories.

Most underprivileged kids, especially from the Deep South or up north, do not get a chance to see beyond their housing projects or small towns. They rarely travel much. Some of them, even if they grow up in Brooklyn and finally visit Manhattan, feel like they might as well be in another country.

One of the best ways to close the achievement gap is through travel. How to do that without a big budget? Try the cheapest and easiest way to travel: read a book. My first time in a European city felt familiar because I had read about it in books years before I ever arrived—what a great feeling!

How can a child say he's bored when there are books ready to read? It's tough to be bored and read a good book at the same time—as long as you have introduced your child to the exciting part of what books can do for them. If you just leave it to the schools to teach your child to read with no model or experiences for them to understand how great books can be, too often they will see reading as schoolwork rather than an adventure.

Make Your Child a Born Reader

Before our children were born, Julius and I would talk, read aloud, and play music for them. I bought the first volume of the Little Golden Books series when I was just three months pregnant. It was a good time for our babies to hear their daddy talk, read, or sing.

After all, they could hear me talk all day long. Lord, I hope they didn't remember some of the things I said.

Anyway, when they came out into this world, we would read some of the same books and play the music again. It's not too early to start with the babies; they seemed to perk up when we read aloud as if they were already familiar with the experience.

The idea of reading to babies before birth has become more common. There is even an adaptation of Dr. Seuss's stories geared to read to your baby before he is born. No matter what, it is good to let your unborn children hear your voices as you read and sing so they can learn to recognize and be calmed by those special sounds.

Be Proud to Read Out Loud

We enjoyed reading aloud to our children. It was a time to focus on them as they listened to the stories. One of my favorites (and, luckily, the kids' favorite too) was *The Three Billy Goats Gruff.* I did all the sound effects for each story as we went along—you know, the hoarse voice of the goats or the birthday candle huff and puff for *The Three Little Pigs.* It was all part of the experience.

MAMA'S MOJO Forget stories you don't like to read (in or out of utero). Your lack of enthusiasm as you read will spoil your efforts. There are some children's books that can get on your last nerve. Just read what you and your child like.

Remember to ask questions as you read—don't interrupt too much or you will lose the movement of the story. For example, pause for a moment and ask why the billy goats were on that bridge, or ask what your child thinks might happen next.

After you have finished, challenge your child to imagine what he would do in the same fix as one of the characters. Like, what would he do if his house were being huffed and puffed to the ground? This teaches a child to connect information and understand appropriate behavior.

When you read aloud, get close to your child. I'd usually sit on the floor and pull some of the kids on my lap. It was such a great chance to get snuggly. I think because I sat on the floor with so many kids, that's why I can still manage to get down on the floor with my grandchildren.

Don't sit across the room and tell a story. Your closeness associates reading with a positive experience. Allow your child to turn the pages of the book as soon as he can. Let him touch the book—while you are nearby—so it becomes familiar.

{ MAMA'S MOJO Don't forget to read the author's and illustrator's names and make sure your child knows what those words mean. Later on, ask a child to be an author or illustrator of a homemade book. }

Just because your kids have learned how to read on their own doesn't mean you should stop reading aloud. That's a great time to ask the kids to read a section of a book to you. It will also make them feel important.

Reading-aloud time is the perfect opportunity to introduce your child, grandchild, or younger brothers and sisters to stories that were meaningful to you when you were their age. I introduced Lola, Chris's daughter, to her daddy's favorite book, *Harry the Dirty Dog* (about a dog who ran away from a bath). Chris shared with his youngest brother his own much-loved Curious George book series.

Have a Family Affair—With Reading

Try to schedule a special reading time for your children. Fit it into your family schedule just like a baseball practice. It can be after church or after dinner. It can be at home, in the backyard, or on the beach. I don't care if your child reads a comic book at first. It will make a difference.

> **MAMA'S MOJO** Here's some bonus mojo: a scheduled reading time for your kids may be the only time you can read a magazine article in peace while your kids read something else.

Encourage your family to exchange ideas about books and articles. When you find something interesting, say, "Hey, listen to this," then read it aloud and talk about it. Ask for an opinion: "What do you think of this idea?" These interactions make it more fun to learn. At the same time, it helps stimulate critical thinking. Besides, the more your kids see you as up on reading, the more they will want to keep on reading!

Get the Power of the Words

Reading will, of course, increase our child's vocabulary—and learning more vocabulary words helps your child to read better and understand what people say. The meaning of an article or program can get lost or at least not fully appreciated if some of the words in it aren't understood.

Tell your child to fill in the blanks. If he listens to someone speak and doesn't understand a word or two, it is no problem **IF** (heavy emphasis on the "if") he finds out about the word. Encourage him to ask the speaker. It is so much better to ask than to remain a dummy. Believe me, no one thinks less of your child. Explain why the speaker will probably think more of your child because it means he wants to learn.

The dictionary is still the big thing if your child sees a word he doesn't know in a book, article, or on TV. Keep a dictionary handy in the house and give a paperback version to your child to carry around. Yes, of course, you should tell your kids about dictionary .com; it is a good definition source while they are on the Internet. But I think nothing beats the actual book form of the dictionary, because while your child is looking up a word and flipping the pages, his attention might fall on another word and then another. He might even decide to start reading the dictionary in search of some new, interesting words. Just a warning: your child might even try to look up and learn words to stump you. So, keep that dictionary handy!

I think every American family should subscribe to *Reader's Digest*—especially if they have school-age children—if only for the Word Power section. That has to be the most magnificent teaching column. If you've not seen it, here's the deal: There are a number of vocabulary words in each section. Go over the words with your child and let him learn the words and the meanings, which are spelled out. You will be surprised at what you have! If they only learn ten words each time, in one year that's 120 new vocabulary words to make reading easier!

Don't Forget Library Power

I have such good memories of the library—it is such a great resource. When I was a girl, I'd go into our school library all the time and check out books. I would rather read than play jump rope during recess. My biggest problem was a timely book return. In my yearbook, a "friend" suggested I'd better return all my overdue books before I graduated.

The local library can be a meaningful place for your kids—especially if you get to know the children's librarian. She can help you figure out what books are best for your kids. She can also tell you about story hours, book clubs, and programs for all ages. She can even give you the inside track through book reviews of new children's books. Your kids will always find something interesting to do.

{ **MAMA'S MOJO** Make it a pleasure trip when
you take the kids to the public library. Pick an easy day

for you. Try to coordinate it with a special program for
the kids. Include a treat on the way home—that way,
the library will be associated with a good time and
exciting possibilities.

Join the Clipper Club for Readers

I must have inherited my clip-mania from my Grandma McClam,
who taught me to read. She would clip articles out of magazines
and papers to read later on or send to the family to read. If I see
inspirational or interesting stuff, I send it. I often send Kenny
goal-oriented materials about how to live your dream. I find something for everyone, clip it, and send it.

Even the littlest kids can get involved; while you clip your articles, let them cut out letters or numbers from magazines and newspapers. They can paste it on paper, or—if they are older—you can
show them how to make a story out of the letters and words they
have clipped out. That keeps them busy and teaches them the
magic of how words go together!

MAMA'S MOJO Here's a great project: clip articles of
interest, poems, pictures, whatever. Paste them on thick,
bunched binder paper and put them in a simple notebook.
Or, use construction paper as a book cover and paste the
article inside. It's a great project for all ages, and you can
create inexpensive, personal "books" for your
family library that way.

Can't Say It? Let a Book Do It for You!

Sometimes, if we parents can't find the right words, we can find the right book (or a magazine article) to read to our kids and say what we need to say. It helps. For example, the book *Leon the Late Bloomer*, by Robert Kraus, is perfect for the middle child who doesn't do things as quickly as the other kids.

With the right, well-chosen books or articles, you don't have to say a thing. They take care of it for you. Tough subjects like bedwetting, moving to a new house, or a new baby can all be approached through books. You don't have to say much because a book will say it all and can often offer you advice on how to proceed. It will certainly offer an opening for discussion with your child.

One time, when Tony wanted a doll, we were guided by the wisdom in *William's Doll*, by Charlotte Zolotow. That book explained about a boy's desire for a doll, how it was not abnormal, and what they did about it. We were able to read about it together as a family with Tony. It opened the discussion, offered answers to all of our questions, and resolved an issue.

You Can Always Count on Comic Books

Comic books helped my generation to read. They often entice reluctant readers—especially boys—even though some people think comic books are just for fun. Well, they are fun, but they also have real literary elements like heroes, characters, and plots. In addition, comics are a great start to read aloud to kids because of those great sound effects: Boof! Bam! Crash!

Not only that, but often slower readers are helped by using a comic's illustrations to accompany what they are reading—what better than a comic with pictures, actions, and more to activate imagination and accelerate reading. A slower reader can actually see what the words mean in terms of visual imagery. That helps him understand what it is so he can apply it to anything he is reading. It helps him learn to imagine. Don't overlook comic books as a terrific reading tool.

And who among us parents can forget our teenage comic stash? My friends and I read the Archie comics. We'd dish about Betty and Veronica, two teenage girls who fought over Archie and Reggie, two teenage boys. We laughed at the characters from the mythical Riverdale High School, especially Jughead Jones and Miss Grundy, a high school teacher.

Reading needs to be fun and interesting to keep your kids coming back for more—especially if they've slowed down on reading or are struggling. Find high-interest materials and keep them coming. Use these strategies to keep your kids on top of their reading game.

Reading Is the Icing on the Cake

Bottom line, we need our kids to read! Reading is *the* great imagination and visualization tool. When a child hears the words or reads to himself, he has to visualize. Imagination requires the ability to *pretend*. Children need to be children. They must explore. We can see what happens to kids who have not developed much imagination—if any—and how that can impede their progress in school and in life. Most often, it is because a child comes from a home where there are no books, where parents don't read or even think reading is important. Such children have often never been to a library or a story hour.

Years back, when I taught school, I saw a classic example of what it meant for a child to have an undeveloped imagination. In our early grade classrooms we had a "housekeeping" section with a miniature stove, refrigerator, and kitchen tools. We had no plastic food like today—our "food" was make-believe. Teachers could tell in such settings which little kids had stories read to them and which kids didn't have that opportunity. The difference seemed to be directly related to their ability to imagine.

A conversation took place between two kids in the class. A little girl was busy whipping up an imaginary cake—one of the assignments. She asked her "partner," a little boy, to get her two eggs from the refrigerator. He opened the little refrigerator and shook his head. "I ain't seen no eggs," he said seriously. She turned to him. "What do you mean?" she said strongly. "We are going to have a fabulous tea party today. I'm going to make this beautiful lemon cake and you are going to help me by getting the eggs."

The bewildered boy said, "I ain't seen no cake or no eggs, either."

How startling and how sad that he did not have the skills necessary to get into that magic moment of creating an imaginary lemon cake (or pretending to eat it at a tea party).

What you and I might see as normal is not normal to many children. There are kids who have never owned a book. I heard about a child who said happily, "Wow, I have two books now!" after receiving a book from a community group.

We need to reach out to these children and get books for them through the communities, the churches, and the schools. Parents, if your child has outgrown his books or if you are able to purchase an extra book or two whenever you buy your child books or magazines, pass that gift along. Teachers, clergy, or anyone who knows about a child without books must help make the community aware of such children. We don't want to let these kids slip through without having the tools to make it in the world.

Imagination is the key to learning and to achieving success as a child or adult. Help your child and all children to imagine the world and to realize it is possible to have your cake and eat it too, through reading.

Think about it for a moment; not only is reading a privilege so many were denied in the past—we have to respect what it means to have the freedom to read whatever we choose. It is a responsibility for people of color to be on the forefront of the best education—and reading ability—for their children and the children of other minorities.

It is also the responsibility of all parents to do whatever they can to support their children to become the best readers they can be. It's not about a parent's income level or educational level—it's about making reading material available (don't forget the "homemade" books from clippings and construction paper, borrowed books, and the resources of the library) in your home. Learning to read and continuing to read is also linked to a family's overall involvement with reading. Show by your example, read aloud, and be proud to help your child achieve.

Reading opens the world to travel, to be up on what's happening in the world, and to discover the world's knowledge and ideas from some of its finest thinkers. It is the ultimate freedom.

Children also learn about people from other walks of life through books. This offers a hope for the future when children learn to understand the world and its people. That is a great hope to combat ignorance, which afflicts society and the world and causes such harm. The world is waiting for all of our children to succeed—we need every one of them.

Remember Mama Rock's Rules and Strategies

- Pass On a Reverence for Reading

  Reading is a privilege many were denied in the past. Have a respect for what it means to enjoy the freedom to read.

- Let Reading Feed Their Imagination

  Reading is the ultimate imagination tool—a key to achieving success as a child or as an adult. Help your children and all children to imagine the world.

- Make Your Child a Born Reader

  Start early for a head start by reading to your child before he is born.

- **Be Proud to Read Out Loud**

  It's critical to read out loud with your child—and a perfect time to bond and give one-on-one attention.

- **Have a Family Affair with Reading**

  Schedule a special reading time for your family—just like any appointment. It will stimulate thinking, promote reading, and create a special family memory.

- **Don't Forget Library Power**

  Take a pleasure trip to the local library. Look to the children's librarian; she is there to help get the most out of available programs.

- **Join the Clipper Club for Readers**

  Clip articles from magazines or newspapers to create a "book" for your family library.

7

Push "Unable"
off the Table

GAVE MY CHILDREN AN ATTITUDE—a "don't quit" attitude. Although I made it clear that it's OK to fail—if you learn from it—or even stop for awhile, it is not OK to give up at the first hint of difficulty. They need to know that life is hard, and struggles are always there, but at the heart of any success is the ability to keep going no matter how tough it is, how rough it might get, or how long it takes. Kids must understand that they will run into obstacles and problems. If they don't, they will get in over their heads at the first big roadblock—or maybe just the first stop sign!

> *Andre: Our mama didn't allow us to say the word "can't." She'd say, "'Can't' is a curse." She told us we could say something is difficult or hard; we could say we needed help with a problem—but, no, "can't" was a "never-say-it" word in our house.*

Parents, we have to get wise and help our children, as soon as we can, to set some goals based on their ages and abilities. Just the act of living day to day requires goals. If we don't help our children to set them, it's like not having any rules—there are no priorities. It's too easy that way for life to become aimless and vulnerable to outside pressures. Goals get your kids through the day and through life. They offer something to aspire to and a game plan to achieve it.

You Have to See a (Real) Man or (Real) Woman to Be a (Real) Man or (Real) Woman

Children can aspire to such goals and sacrifice through your example. When sacrifice is in your home, let them know. But there is a fine line between keeping family sacrifices to yourself and letting it all hang out—you know the type of martyr parents who repeat daily how much they've given up for their children. Julius and I let our kids know matter-of-factly when we sacrificed our time and effort for something our family wanted or needed.

Julius would mention, "OK, Mommy is working two hours later each night to get that extra whatever—so your job is to help with some of her tasks." Or I'd say, "Daddy took on an extra job for six months so we could go on that family trip we have been counting on. That's why he's not home tonight, and you are responsible for helping around the house."

This gave the children a chance to appreciate what each parent should do for the family. They get the reality lesson: they are not entitled and everything does not magically come to them. They see that hard work is what makes it all happen. I say: "You have to see a (real) man to be a (real) man." My boys needed to see their father act like a man and take care of his family, his work, and his life so they could have a model.

The same holds true for the needs of girls to "see a (real) woman to be a (real) woman." That can happen with the right mama in the house.

Andre: I understand things since I've become a father. As a kid growing up, I never saw our refrigerator without food or our house without heat. My father began his workday at 4 A.M. Nothing stopped him from making his life and our life work. He always planned. When I was in college, someone thought I must be rich because I didn't need financial aid. No, my dad knew when I was born that I was going to college, so he started saving.

Do It Right and It Will Be Alright!

Kids want you to praise them and see good things. Remember to start early, even when your child is a few months old, to mold and teach him acceptable behavior. You teach them what you expect so they know what to do. I think it is the greatest thing about raising kids: the chance to instill in them everything you want them to achieve (even when they are not with you). I've been told that the reason my kids are successful is because I expected no less from

Ann: There were always children in and out of 619 Decatur Street. It was a haven for any child, no matter what the problem—or even if she had no problems. Kids would come socialize and look for guidance and directions from a mother who knew how to fix everything. Parents and youths of the "day" knew there was nothing Mama Rock couldn't do (she is still that way). Who could believe such power could be pent up in such a small frame? But it is—she is a strong tower of strength for all of us.

them. My theory is that, more often than not, they will give you just what you expect. Your faith in them is the key to unlock their potential. Be a guiding force to bring the best out of them—do it right and it will be alright.

Children Need to Know *Whose* They Are

All that being said, children should be taught who they are and *whose* they are. Each one is a child of God. Children should understand they are wondrously made because God doesn't make junk. Therefore, no one can say to a child: "You are nothing. You'll never be anything."

Anyone remember Art Linkletter's *Kids Say the Darndest Things* show? Young kids would be asked questions and they'd answer honestly (because they knew no other way). Oh yes, they'd say the *darndest* things! Once, Mr. Linkletter asked a little boy what his mother always said to him. The boy paused, and then answered, "My mommy always says I ain't worth s—t!"

You tell me, what would motivate that child to get out there and do something when his mother told him he is not worth s—t? **Here it is:** if anyone, anywhere in his world, could encourage and build up a child, miracles could happen.

Do you know the story of Antwone Fisher, the successful author and film producer? His personal trauma began when he was born to an incarcerated teenager and then placed in the foster care of a physically and verbally abusive "parent." She ranted over and over to him: "You come from nothing, you ain't nothing, and you are never going to be nothing."

He had a hard time relating to people after he left home to join the navy. One officer noticed Antwone always finished last in everything. He took it upon himself to compliment him. "Good job!" he would say as Antwone ran by on military exercises. The officer kept up his praise, and soon Antwone was in the lead—yes!

After the navy, while he worked as a security guard at Sony Pictures Studio, a producer heard his life story. Out of that beginning, the movie *Antwone Fisher* was eventually made (he wrote the screenplay).

That story emphasizes this important truth: if someone will encourage a young person, like the naval officer who complimented Antwone, it often begins a transformation, and miracles can be achieved—just like his. I'm happy to tell you that today, Antwone has a beautiful family. Most of all, I'm pleased to tell you that he located his former foster mother. He explained his successful life to her and said, "and YOU told me I would be nothing." Then, he turned and walked away. He never spoke with her again. He didn't have to. He had lived the truth—and let her know—that no one can ever tell a child he is nothing or will never be anything and be SURE it will stick. Especially not when others are there to support and help those who just need some encouragement to be a success.

Get Wise and Prioritize

When I spoke recently with a school group, some of the kids asked me what Chris was doing. They wanted to know what car he drove or what was his next movie? I told those kids it was more important what *they* wanted to do instead of what somebody else does, like Chris.

Kids shouldn't focus on what someone else is doing—especially those who are famous—they need to set their own goals. I explained to those kids that their first priority was to set a goal and then to figure out how they were going to accomplish it.

Young people are bombarded with so much crap on TV that many honestly think life is all about cars and money. Peer pressure and marketers are always at it, pushing kids to want more and more. But I've never once heard anyone talk about actual blueprints to achieve all those wonderful things.

We parents also need to point out that success is not always who makes the money, either. It could be Mr. Jones down the street who has six children and maintains his family and home by hard work. Children are so often exposed to wonderful role models—they just don't recognize them. They are so busy looking for someone larger than life or for some fancy person that they don't see the real deal in front of their faces. Teach your children to see the worth of ordinary people—people who might not fit into the TV image—who are successful at what they do despite the odds they continue to face every day.

Get Real About Role Models

One of Chris's jokes says a lot about how many people view who is honored these days. He said, "If you get a master's degree, people say that's good—if you get out of prison, they throw you a big party."

When did our society start to glorify celebs who did something wrong or make criminals into celebrities? What about these "role model" stars that shoplift, carry guns, and indulge in other bad behavior, who get all kinds of press coverage—and are often applauded (and celebrated)? They seem to be presented as "cool" or something to emulate; anyway, they get lots of press.

At the same time, not enough is done to celebrate the achievement of educational or career goals. We need to get behind completions and graduations for our children. We need to throw a party for their high school diploma, their cosmetology certificate, as well as their PhD. It really doesn't matter, because all of these achievements are about your child reaching his personal career goal.

During a recent address to high school students, I asked some of the kids in the audience what they wanted to be. A young

Mervin "Spectac" Jenkins: If I walk into a school, probably the first thing I'll see is a sign congratulating the school for the best ball team or other sports victory. I've yet to see a banner imprinted with "congrats for the highest academic achievement around." Our society says, "It's all about academics." Really? Then why are sports stars getting umpteen dollars and a college professor—well, you know he's not getting that. We need to get society motivated to respect the power of education on all levels, and, of course, we need to start with our students to do the same.

man spoke up. He wanted to be an auto mechanic. There was a burst of laughter. I paused for a few moments until the laughter had died down. "Listen up," I told the kids, "if this young man has a goal to be a *good* auto mechanic you need to use your imagination; suppose he could work at one of those Mercedes, BMW, or Jaguar plants—think of how well he could do." I also reminded the group of the money to be made if he had his own auto repair business. After all, everybody needs their car fixed sometime, don't they?

Welcome Dreams to the Light of Day

You can encourage your children from the beginning to talk about their personal dreams. Start as soon as your child says, "When I grow up I want to be a . . ." and continue to encourage what he aspires to do. It's important to listen and be there to offer advice and direction at the beginning and during all the starts and stops on the road to success.

Too often, our schools focus on what's not as good about a child rather than what outstanding abilities a child does have (especially if the child is not academic). Offer some adaptable expectations for anything your child wants to achieve. If your child is talented in the arts—or likes to sew, cook, or build—encourage him to talk about what he projects to achieve in such fields and help him see it happen.

For example, a child who likes to cook has a wide-open field in the culinary arts. He or she could be a personal chef, an executive chef, or the owner of a catering company. Maybe your son wants to be a hairdresser or a barber. Don't stop there. Help him envision a salon, his own shop, or a position as a makeup artist for a TV studio or even a movie star. Does your daughter whip up her own clothes with ease and design some for her friends? Check out the possibilities—we can always use another Donna Karan. That's how it all starts. There are no limits to what your child can do.

> { **MAMA'S MOJO** Share your childhood dreams with your children and grandchildren. Talk about what stopped you from achieving them or how you ended up living your dream. These are important discussions. They are the perfect chance to help your children decide if their goals are realistic. If so, you can help them plan what steps they can take to get there. }

Yes, Big Strong Trees Start with a Little Acorn

I often explain how to start with small goals. I share the various steps needed to reach specific goals and the work involved. For example, if a recent high school graduate just started as an entry-level secretary, he or she could work up to an administrative position. Soon, with the right education, it is possible to achieve a management position and more.

There are so many higher education options today and even more scholarships and student loans to make them possible.

No one can say he is unable to attend college or technical school—please. There are so many possibilities, such as online degree programs or flexible classes or credits given for life experience, that the door is wide open for an education.

When I look back, I realize my kids didn't always end up as I thought they would. I expected Chris would work for a big newspaper because he could take ten spelling words and use them to produce a ten-page essay. I imagined he might get serious and win a literature prize. When he started in broadcast journalism, I figured he'd be the next Frankie Crocker—a legendary original, a hip and flamboyant radio personality.

I was sure Brian was going to be a doctor; he even studied pre-med. Instead of going that way, he went into the ministry as an avocation and the corporate business world as a vocation.

Andre and Tony would be schoolteachers, I assumed. Andre started out in the school system. He was so good with kids, and they loved him. Today, he owns his own company, Julius Rock Trucking Company. Tony has found his niche in acting and comedy.

Surely our super sportswoman, Ally, was going to the Olympics and then into a career as a professional athlete. A little accident sidetracked her, so she ended up in academia as a cross-country coach and a college professor. (At least someone became a teacher.)

Kenny is a work in progress. He is my starving actor, self-sufficient and independent. I know whatever he does, he will continue to be a success.

Andrea ("Andi") is at Winthrop College majoring in broadcast journalism. I think Andi is funnier than Chris and Tony put together. I see her as a thinking woman's comic.

Jordan is definitely going to follow in the comic footsteps—the bug has already bitten him.

Ann has such a caring gift for ministering to people—her career as a social worker is right on target.

Who knows what the future will bring in terms of career paths for my children or yours? If we listen carefully to the dreams of their hearts, help them learn from their mistakes, and keep up our encouragement, we support them toward success.

Failure Should Be the Ultimate Motivator

We need to support our kids as a work in progress from the day they are born. Everything takes time. There will be lots of starts and stops and even some failures before they get near that finish line.

In our family, *we are allowed to fail.* There is no shame in failure. Sometimes, not succeeding at something means it is time to regroup. Other times, it could mean our child wasn't on the right path.

Failure should be the ultimate motivator for a child. It can push him back on the right track and get him going. Tell your child: real failure is in not trying to start over. It is in not dusting yourself off and finding the right path to the success that is out there.

Your child should not let failure take him down; he can still go after what he wants with a new resolve. After all, some of the most successful people in the world today and in the past have experienced big-time failures (that could be a whole book by itself). Real success can be found inside failure if a child analyzes what went wrong and finds a solution to it. If children can see failure as a learning experience, they won't be afraid.

Push "Unable" off the Table

Forget the *blame game* of circumstances like race, religion, poverty, or physical limitation as blocks to success. Blaming one's circumstances has nothing to do with success or failure. If you are poor and use that as an excuse—forget it. Poverty should be your motivation to get the hell out of it, to change your life. People say, "But I live in the projects, so how can I . . ." Well, move on. Projects were meant to be temporary. The idea was to move in so money could be saved to move out and up. They were not meant to be ancestral homes for generations going nowhere.

Don't blame race—black is a color, not a condition—for your child's lack of success (or even your own). To say you can't do something because you are black is to demean what successful black people have accomplished.

If physical limitation becomes an excuse not to pursue success, it is an insult to so many disabled people who have done wonders—like Helen Keller, who became blind and deaf after a childhood illness and

Ann: One of the most important things I learned from Mama Rock was this: if someone from another race or culture attacked my character or reputation in any way, I should carry myself above reproach so that even the attacker would be ashamed for the wrong they had done or the shame they had tried to bring to me. I also learned to prove them a liar by my actions and to always strive beyond what was expected of me.

went on to attend college and become an activist for workers' rights. Think about Harriet Tubman, who suffered from epilepsy yet dedicated her life to civil rights and women's suffrage. Designer Tommy Hilfiger played the class clown in school so no one would find out about his learning problems, but that did not stop him from becoming world famous.

Stop making excuses for your children or letting them justify failures. It's always the right time to push "unable" off your table and help your children—and all children—go after their rightful place in the world.

Leave Your Background Behind

The only limits a child has are the ones he puts on himself because there are *no limits*. Your child can do anything, and parents, so can you. So many people think their background defines them. Listen, there wouldn't be any Oprah or so many other great people if this were the case.

Don't hold responsible the fact that a child is orphaned or fostered as a reason for him not to be successful. Such a thought would fly in the face of such accomplished people as President Andrew Jackson, whose father died soon after he was born and who became orphaned at fourteen years old.

Look around—there are so many stories of people who have achieved greatness from humble beginnings and so many others who have had setbacks, problems, and situations but triumphed over them all. Find examples of such people in the newspaper or on TV and talk about it with your children. Read biographies and autobiographies—including children's books—about such examples. Don't hesitate to point out these people whenever you can.

Don't Quit, Stick with It!

Before your child ever begins anything, deliver the expectation that you require him to stick with it. There are ways to develop your child's staying power. Start with this: don't set your child up for something without checking it out. For example, don't pay for a semester of karate lessons for your daughter just because her friend did it. Instead, set up a trial session and see if she even likes it! If you don't do that, you can't expect to make her stick with it—especially if it's not for her.

However, once your child decides to do something, and you've gone through the "trial period," don't let him think he's entitled to quit the minute anything gets tricky or tough. At worst, he will establish a pattern of quitting lessons, school, even relationships. Anyway, unless he learns to stick with it, how will he ever develop patience and the other skills necessary to finish what he started?

This is true even when your kids are older. For example, your teenage daughter has a goal to earn extra money for college. Great! Be sure to sit down with her to make certain she understands the steps to take. Let her know that a concrete plan should be devised with a backup plan for the setbacks that will surely happen. Help her understand that—just like everything else your child has learned—there are the details she must attend to before moving on to the next phase. The big picture is great, but the details can get in the way if they are not accounted for in a solid plan. If you have been consistent before now, she'll know you expect her to stay with what she starts. Hopefully **she** will expect herself to stay with it because she has learned that is the way to success in anything.

Build a House of Praise

One time Andre's teacher sent home a note for a teacher conference—with no other explanation. The day of the meeting, she related an exercise she had done in his class. Each kid was asked to share what their parents said about them; she told us 95 percent of the kids in her class repeated something negative. She quickly added that Andre was another story; he didn't hesitate to say, "My mother thinks I'm the greatest thing there is!" She wanted to meet the parents of a kid who had that much confidence. Listen, anytime a child's parents think he is wonderful, the child is going to fight to prove them right. Some kids do the wrong thing because they rationalize: *my parents think I'm a loser, so, why fight it?* Be careful what you say—do your best to think of another way to convey your thoughts if you are disappointed in your child.

Know What You Came to Do

Julius always had a sports story to illustrate a concept or lesson for the children and their friends. One of his better stories was about Hank Aaron when he played for the Yankees and Yogi Berra was the third-base coach. Yogi—according to the way Julius told the story—instructed Hank to hold the bat with the label forward so he could get a better hit. Hank looked at Yogi, walked up to the plate, grabbed the bat his own way, and knocked the ball out of the park. Afterward, he said to Yogi, "I came here to get a home run, not a hit."

Help your children understand that they need to do their best in their own way. They need to think big, have dreams, and trust their own abilities. If they have the faith to do what they think they are really capable of doing, then outside influences will not distract them from what they came to do: to be as outstanding as they can be at whatever they choose to do, large or small.

Be a Substitute Teacher at the "Dropout Factories"

What happened? At one time, sharecroppers, farmers, and migrant workers had to take their children out of school to pick cotton or fruit or to work the fields. Kids had to start to school late or leave early in different seasons. At a certain age, some kids had to drop out entirely because the family needed them desperately to work on the farm or in town to keep everything afloat.

Many of these children swore their offspring would not have to experience what they had. So, they pushed their children and grandchildren to school, and many graduated from college.

Today, there is freedom to go to school without that kind of interruption, but so many kids don't want to take advantage of it. Some parents don't step up and demand the best because they don't hold the schools accountable. We need to push schools to be accountable, especially for creating high school graduates. A solid education is a strong key to being able to achieve success in this world. It is the great equalizer of opportunity.

A Johns Hopkins researcher, Bob Balfanz, coined a nickname for high schools where 40 percent or more of the students never made it to their senior year. He nicknamed these schools "Dropout Factories." The awful part is that at least one in every ten schools in this country could fit that description.

Some people with money just pull their kids out of the public schools into charter or private schools. This is not the way to *enable* a generation of children. Certainly not a generation that needs—at the most basic level—for as many people as possible to have a high school diploma.

Literacy programs are full of forty- and fifty-year-olds who can't read. Why on earth is that? Now, a ninety-year-old who can't read, that is understandable given that generation. What happened to the parents who had a sixth-grade education and pushed their

Kenny: I don't feel that I'm necessarily better than someone else because of the family I grew up with. I guess I was left with the responsibility to teach my friends some strategies on how to live and be independent. Sometimes I feel like I'm in a world of my own because of my values. I'm not trying to be bigger or better—I just want to hold onto those core values while I succeed at doing what I came to do.

kids to do so much better? My mother-in-law raised fourteen successful children because she pushed them. She didn't have the education, but she made sure her children did. Today, we have generations where mother and grandmother don't care about higher education at all.

This is a responsibility for everyone, not only parents of school-age children. These are America's children and we are all accountable. Parents, remember this: you are your child's first teachers and the ultimate teachers. If your school does not teach black history, do it at home. If the school did not assign James Baldwin's or Dick Gregory's books, get them for your child and make sure he reads them.

If you are of Irish heritage and the school does not mention the history of the famine in your homeland—get the books and read them together with your children. Latino history, Native American history, whatever religion or nationality reflects your family—teach that heritage to your children. Let them know who they are to give them the confidence to succeed.

Jump in there and help if your kids are having problems at school. When your kids go into preschool they are supposed to know certain things because you should have taught them. If you don't know what they are, ask someone. Good resources include local preschools, kindergarten teachers, and libraries. Many can recommend programs like Hooked on Phonics or other programs available at little or no charge from libraries and literacy groups.

Chris says: "If Johnny can't read, blame his mother. If there are no lights in his house to read, blame the daddy." It is up to us parents to make sure that the basics are met.

Embrace the "H" Word

Homework—that big, bad "H" word—is inevitable. It is also one of the flash points toward a child's ultimate success or failure. It is definitely the most important thing you can help your child to master. However, the discipline and commitment needed to get a grip on homework can foster hot-tempered emotional exchanges in a family. Parents feel guilty or resentful if they have to help too much, are too "busy" to help, or—worse—if their child expects them to do all the work. If the kids end up being nagged, they turn sullen and angry. The result is that both parents and kids feel miserable—and no homework gets done!

> **MAMA'S MOJO** Whatever you do, don't tell your kids you hated math or science homework. What a great excuse for them to throw that back at you. There's nothing cute in saying you are a third-generation math moron—even when it is true! Keep that kind of information—and any other mistakes you made that you didn't fix—to yourself! Now, juicy failures that you triumphed over—like how you brought a bad grade up to an A+—tell about them right now.

When your child first starts to get homework, develop a game plan and stay with it. Set the stage for when and where he will do his homework—kitchen table, a bedroom desk, or near your "at-home" office. Wherever you decide, organize a place and set it up with everything you need—pencils, paper, and all. We had a tremendous island in the center of the kitchen on Decatur Street. I could cook on one side and my children could line up to do homework on the other side. I could walk down the aisle, check the homework, and offer a little help, if needed. The kids knew I was available to help—but I wouldn't do their homework for them (besides, most teachers know exactly what's going on).

Take the chore out of homework when you can. Remember how your little kids were thrilled to do "big kids' work"? Let your younger children (even in preschool) sit at the table or area assigned for homework with their older siblings. Even if they can only color or read a comic book, let them do this as often as possible.

Do What You Dread and Get Ahead

Stress this to your children: do the hardest thing first. This approach to homework will help them in everything they do in life. Let them do what they dread most right off the bat. Treat homework like you do other chores or assignments. Tell your kids that when homework is done, they can move on to something they want to do.

> **MAMA'S MOJO** Ask about homework assignments. Don't accept "I dunno" or "I don't have any." Get positive, ask your child if he has any questions before you begin. That's the time to check it out—not by interrupting everyone when there is something basic you could have fixed before he started to do the wrong assignment or complete it the wrong way.

My expectations were high. Although I never said my kids had to be all "A" students, they were expected to do their best. I didn't want my children to think it was acceptable to turn in something "barely passable." Yes, I was one of those mamas who said to my kid when he got a 97 percent on a test: "Good work, but what happened to the other three points?" Here's the thing: if I let it go and don't ask about it, then next time they might miss two more. It's critical what you do with that. Stop it in the beginning, don't let it perpetuate. Ask them what you need to do *to help them* make it all the way to 100 percent—and then do it!

You had better believe all the things you share with the kids about how to improve their homework (don't procrastinate, do the work neatly and on time, and all those other good habits) will influence their abilities in the workforce and everywhere else. It will influence them all their lives.

Yes, like so many other things we have talked about, good parenting takes time. Fostering good study and life habits while serving as a homework guide to your child takes time. If you set it up right with an optimistic attitude, you'll spend less time on that dreaded "H" word.

Beware of Turning Out Cookie-Cutter Children

There's still another side to making your child a success that is not talked about enough. Your child is not a mini version of you—to put that on a child is unfair. If you harbor unreasonable expectations for your kids, it can lead to serious problems—yours and theirs. Even in the same family, kids can have completely different skills. Kenny and Andi were good writers, so everyone expected Jordan to be the same. But he's not them; he doesn't even like the same things. I cannot expect him to "be" them—and I don't. He has other talents, and that is what I continue to encourage.

Some parents try to use their children to make themselves feel better about who they are. They expect their children, as they get older, to choose what they have chosen as a life path or take a certain direction that the parent feels will enhance his or her own sense of self-esteem. Parents, please don't look to your kids to validate who you are. You need to validate who *they* are and make them do the best they are able to do. Get to know your children and what they can achieve—look into their hearts and spirits. When you were new parents, you could look down at your infant and imagine he could do anything. You might think your baby could be the hope of the free world. Later on, that scenario may be a faraway memory. Keep that positive reinforcement going, though, even if you have to smile through your fears.

> **MAMA'S MOJO** Don't compare your child's behavior
> to one of your other kids or the neighbor down the block.
> Each child is a glorious individual who should be raised as the
> best he can be. Don't make him act or aspire to be like
> someone else if it doesn't fit, because that sets him up
> for failure. Lose these questions: "Why can't you be more
> like your big sister?" or "Why don't you clean up
> your room like your brother?"

Outside the home, teachers and relatives put the squeeze on your kids to be the same type of athlete, actress, or math ace as their sibling was. Don't add to that burden. Help your kids clarify who they are. With my kids, everyone was different. We accepted it and celebrated each child for who he or she was.

If your children are aware of a good family reputation, it can help put the brakes on downsliding. Chris had this funny thing; at an early age, he would walk around and say, "I'm Chris Rock." We didn't know what that meant at the time. Looking back, I think it translated into: "I am a child of Julius and Rose Rock, I'm not allowed to do what other people do—I'm expected to do my best."

Andre: My parents didn't tell us we were just as good as someone else. They told us we were better! That worked for us. The more they expected, the more they got what they expected. One time my kids were acting up about homework. All of a sudden, I said, "Rose Rock would not have this!" I had to laugh—I was passing it on to another generation.

Everyone Can't Be a Ballerina

Remember this: not everything your children do is top of the line. Some of it doesn't even meet the halfway mark. While you need to be complimentary, especially as the kids get older, you are not helping if you pump them up in the wrong direction (especially if it is because it's what YOU want them to do).

Some parents have unrealistic expectations. Parents who were always good in math or sports for some reason think their kids will automatically be the same way. Listen, often one kid in the

[MAMA'S MOJO What do people outside the family
say about your child? Do they talk about how funny he is?
Does he tell "yo' mama" jokes from street corners any
chance he gets—and everyone laughs? Does your daughter
throw together outfits and end up looking like she came
off the pages of a fashion magazine? Does everyone tell
you how stylish she is? Listen carefully and look to discover
what you need to know about your child's talents.]

Mervin "Spectac" Jenkins: When I was trying to break into the music industry, I talked to Chrissy. He listened carefully and told me, if I was serious, I should drop everything and move to NYC or LA. Then, his next words cut me to the quick: "If you ask me, Spec, I think you should continue teaching." I thought: here he is doing his big comedian thing and he tells me to teach. Then he said, "You don't have to give up your rap music to do education." You know, it was the best advice I ever got.

family loves sports while another kid can't even pass a ball. Discover the passion of the one child who needs to find out what he is good at and let him run with it. As you concentrate on his strengths and real talents, it will be easier to be openly and honestly supportive of what he is trying to achieve.

I remember one of my teachers whose niece attended our school. For whatever reason, she wanted her niece to excel—she imagined she would be smarter than anyone in the school. Unfortunately, the girl was an average student who was overburdened by such unrealistic expectations. She almost had a nervous breakdown.

If your daughter would rather jump rope than become a ballerina—let her do it, because not everybody can be a ballerina.

"Spec" told me he often thinks about what Chris said to him that day. Now he gets paid to go around the state to tell his story and do rap music—including the spontaneous songs he is known for. He said he thought about all the shows he did as a hip-hop artist sweating hard for an audience that was mostly drunk or high. Now he gets to perform for students and give them a positive message. "It doesn't hurt to take home plenty of money each time I do this, either," he said. Fact is, kids love it when their principal can rap. It gives them a whole new perspective on success. Not only that, but his example can teach the ideals of education and goals in a medium kids can relate to and understand.

Pass It On When They Have Gone

Many parents sacrificed to send a child to school with the understanding that when she graduates, she will help to send the next one in line. Everyone worked as a family to do it. This happened all over to Southern blacks and to immigrants from all religions and nationalities. It was what was done. The idea was to "pass it on." Each of the children had a responsibility to open the door for the next person in the family or community. If that person didn't have enough sense to come in, we'd have to snatch them up and jerk them right in the door. We all need to pass it on today. We need to know what we came to do. If that can happen, as Chris says, perhaps all Americans will have the same opportunities, not just the same chain stores.

Remember Mama Rock's Rules and Strategies

- **You Have to See a Real Man/Woman to Be a Real Man/Woman**

  Children need to realize the value of work and sacrifice to achieve success. Show them a role model for real men and women. Don't play martyr or "hide" necessary compromises.

- **Kids Need to Know Who They Are and "Whose" They Are**

  No one can tell a child he is nothing—because God doesn't make junk.

- **Build a House of Praise**

  Create confident, resilient children with encouragement and praise. They'll try to prove you right.

- **Be a "Substitute" Teacher at the "Dropout Factories"**

  If your child's school isn't teaching what it should, get busy and do it yourself for your child. You are your child's first and ultimate teacher, and our schools need help.

- **Embrace the "H" Word**

  Homework is one of the most important things to help your child master. The same skills learned through doing the "H" word apply to life's lessons and prepare him for success.

- **Beware of Turning Out Cookie-Cutter Children**

  Each child is a glorious individual. Don't compare him to the kid down the street or try to make him into a copy of a sibling or a parent.

- **Everyone Can't Be a Ballerina**

  Measure the reality of parental expectations when you get to know your child's heart, spirit, strengths, and talent.

{ 8 }

Don't Lie Down
with Anything
You Don't Want to
Live with Forever

KIDS DON'T WANT TO HEAR parents talk about sex—they
don't even think we have sex. But we can set them straight
about those birds and those bees. Most important, we
can let them know that sex lasts much longer than a fleeting
moment of sweet commotion. Listen up: if your child isn't careful, he or she may end up with something they'll have to live
with forever.

For our kids, sex is all about physical attraction and a notch
on a belt or a bracelet on the wrist to show off. We parents

know better. We need to step up and share how it should be: special and meaningful. So let's just get straight to it—this means that you need to be open and honest with your kids about sex.

There's no time like right now to have *The Talk*. If your child hasn't asked questions yet, look for a good opportunity to bring it up (at least by the time they are twelve years old). If a relative or friend is expecting a baby, it's a great time—if your child is at least eight years old—to begin a talk about her new, bigger "tummy" and how it got there.

Always let your kids know it is OK to ask about whatever is on their minds from the earliest years. Encourage them to be curious about everything, including sex. Don't panic at a question, though, and simply shut down. All you have to do is answer correctly and use the age-appropriate terms. When your five-year-old asks you where babies come from, he doesn't really want to know. Tell him the name of the local hospital or point out a house down the street with a new baby. When a twelve-year-old child asks you, explain the entire thing from start to finish. Be sure to use correct words like sperm and intercourse. It's not the time to be cute.

Listen, sex education is not a backstage pass to have sex. My motto is: *less talk means more action*. Studies show that teen pregnancy, STDs, and emotional problems are highest in the groups where sex was never discussed. Get up your nerve! Quit hiding from *The Talk*. Steal my strategies and try out some of my *Mama's Mojo* to help you along the way. Trust me, you'll be glad you did.

Mama Rock's Triple-Threat Sex Advice

#1. Parents Know Best

Answers to questions like "why do I wake up with my penis being big?" or "how come I have hair down there when I didn't before?" should not fall into the clutches of brothers and sisters who might make those answers an opportunity for a bad, dirty joke. Please, don't let them get there first. If you do, your kids will soon expand their dirty talk vocabulary and misinformation madness during sleepovers, at the movies, or in secret discussions with their friends.

Of course, kids can still learn from their older brothers and sisters, but mostly about what *not* to do! My son Brian learned plenty about dating blunders from his big brother Chris, who was eight years older. He saw some slip-ups from Andre, who was six years older, and even learned plenty from brother Tony, who was only four years older. He told me he learned the most about what a good romantic relationship could be from Julius and me.

#2. Don't Just Talk About Sex, Talk About Responsibility

I never talk about sex without talking about responsibility and relationships. Kids think sex is a recreational sport and their parents are not in the game. But, hey, the reason sex is so personal is because it is meant to be between people who love and care for each other, and who also want to take responsibility for each other and for the children they create.

Sex is serious business with lifetime consequences. No one should do it because someone else did it (or said they did). It's beautiful and wonderful because it's ordained by God—that's why it's so damn good.

Let your children understand—if they truly love someone, there is a responsibility for that person. Just the act of sex carries a responsibility—more on that later. You ask your kids: "Do you want to hurt your partner?" You ask your girls: "Do you love your boyfriend? You do? Well, how would he feel if irresponsible sex led to an unwanted pregnancy?"

Make your daughter visualize what such a pregnancy would mean to her future. What would happen to her life plans? And what about her guy's plans to go to college on a football scholarship or his dreams of being an actor? Tell her, "Girl, you can kiss them goodbye. Basically, your boyfriend's ability to pursue more than new fatherhood responsibilities is shot."

Ask your boys: "What about your girlfriend's reputation and future if she becomes pregnant? What if one of you ends up with HIV or another sexually transmitted disease?"

Help your kids think hard about the future before they hop into bed. It doesn't only happen to someone else—it can happen to your child. One fleeting moment can last a lifetime.

#3. Don't Worry About "Tell and Do"

When I gave my teenage son a condom, I was not saying it was "sex time." It meant his mama wanted him to have a condom if he planned to have sex—whether Mama liked it or not. At least my sons would have a fighting chance against a sexually transmitted disease or an illegitimate child if they used a condom. You know I'd rather my daughter practice birth control instead of suffering the high cost of not using it if she planned to have sex anyway—and you know her mama wouldn't like that.

I hear people say all the time how they can't believe "whoever" took their fifteen-year-old to get birth control. Come on, today it's just responsible parenting. Pretend all you want that your kid doesn't do this or that—but if they do it anyway, protection is real handy.

> MAMA'S MOJO Even if your child drops a sexual
> bomb on you about something shocking, surprising, or just
> plain bad news—stay cool and controlled. It's out on the
> table already, so let your child know you can be counted on
> to talk openly, no matter what he tells you. Figure out how
> or why this thing happened so you can prevent it from
> happening again—or to another child in the family.

Don't Lie Down with Anything You Don't Want to Live with Forever

I raised my sons and my daughters to be responsible with their bodies. I taught them about the consequences of making a commitment based entirely on scx. After all, what if you can barely have a conversation with this person? What if you find out you don't share any values or morals, or even enjoy the same activities

You Can't Wear a Paternity Suit

I won't tell you which one, but when one of my sons was in high school, a girl decided she was going to have a baby for "Chris Rock's brother." (Chris had become famous at this point.) Isn't that something? They went out together and I guess the deed was done. Within two weeks or so, she announced she was expecting. My son was upset. Of course, I suspected otherwise. Believe me, I took over and laid out the reality: I told her my son gets $1.25 for lunch every day from me, that's it! She would not get anything more from our family. If she could buy Pampers and milk with lunch money, good luck. That was the last we ever heard from her.

Fame can definitely lead to paternity troubles. Professional athletes and celebrities run into the same problems as regular guys if they wind up with an illegitimate child—they've just got more money, and that's when things get tangled. But paternity is not only about the money. If any father is not a right-there father, the child loses out no matter how much cash or fame he has.

except going to bed with each other? It is unbelievably important to be selective about who you want to have your children.

For the Boys

I tell my sons: it is not about sowing wild oats. Imagine you meet a girl and decide to date her. You don't have real feelings for her as yet. You are not "in love" or anything, but the opportunity to have sex comes up and you act on that opportunity.

Fast Forward. Your girl calls with news—she's pregnant. OK, a child is brought into the world by a girl you barely know. Son, you sure won't have the kind of meaningful connection with her that a solid, loving relationship offers, that's for sure.

Fast Forward. Now you are about to leave school or go off in the world. You leave this person and the baby behind to go off to pursue your own life.

Brian: My mother helped me understand why I would want to be with someone who understands that raising our kids is the hardest job in the world. She helped me to know why my partner should complement me with her own goals and ambitions.

Forward again to when you've met "the one" —the girl you love. You get married and start your family. Sure, that's wonderful, but remember you are still connected with that other woman and your child. For one thing, you'll have a legal and financial responsibility until that child is eighteen years old. For another, you'll be the daddy of a child who will be looking in from the outside at your happy life—and he is not part of it.

Women know that it isn't easy for a man to commit. I laughed when my son Chris said, "Every man has to settle down eventually. You know why? Because he doesn't want to end up as 'the old guy' in the club. Every club you go into, there's always some old guy. He ain't really old, just a little too old to be in that club."

I don't want my boys to become the club's "old guy"—the one who keeps looking for the casual sexual relationships that are far from casual in terms of consequences. I want my boys to live a real man's life with their own loving families. To lie down with anyone they don't want to live with forever can create permanent consequences. HIV, STDs, and unwanted pregnancies, all these can keep your children from a full life.

For the Girls

I tell my daughters: sex is far too serious to just "do it" because your girlfriends did it (or said they did it). Girls, if you really love someone and care enough about him to have sex, you are responsible for him too.

So, you meet a nice guy. You don't have deep feelings for him yet—just strong physical ones. You are not *in love* or anything, but the opportunity to have sex comes up and you act on that opportunity.

Fast Forward. You miss your period. Tests confirm your pregnancy. You are now about to bring a child into the world with someone you never loved—and maybe don't even know too well. If he stays involved with your child, you will be connected with him for the rest of your life. Think about that!

Fast Forward. It's about the time you would leave for college or go off to pursue your dreams. The problem is: you probably can't because you have the responsibility of a child.

Fast Forward. You try to meet a good man who understands and accepts that you already have a child. Finally, you do meet such a man and get married. Terrific! But, perhaps in the back of your mind is the worry that he will favor the children you have together more than your first child. You'll also have to contend with another woman when the child's father marries, if he even sees your child. You will also have to stand by as you witness the pain and resentment your child will feel from being on the outside. It's always the children who end up hurt by a parent's poor choices.

Take the "F" out of Romance

Face it, the "F" word is the most common word used in movies. That's because it is the way people talk today. There was a time when a man would not swear in front of a woman in public—those days are over!

The old days relied heavily on innuendo. In classic movies, a man and a woman would kiss and the scene would fade out. Today, the scene never fades out, it keeps rolling.

There was plenty of innuendo in raucous songs like The Rolling Stones' "(I Can't Get No) Satisfaction." Maybe that's why it was so popular—we all knew what it really meant. Now, Snoop Dogg has a song with the lyrics "I want to love you tonight." But if you listen to the unedited version (and everyone does) you'll hear: "I want to 'F' you tonight." Those choice words boom out of open car windows all the time. Do some parents bother to hear what's being said?

Childhood and innocence are taken away by the highly sexualized media muddle. Nothing is sacred. Where are the flowers? The anticipation? Having sex with a different guy or girl every other day is not something to be proud of—no matter what you see on TV or in the tabloids.

When our children give up their bodies to be popular, it's a sad state we are living in—but that's where we live. I just watched a man on the Oprah show who hired a stripper to get butt naked at his fourteen-year-old son's birthday party. Whoever would have thought about something like that? I think in that case, the child must change places and be the parent because his father sure wasn't thinking right.

My son Brian believes almost everyone wants romance even as almost everyone says it is supposed to be dead. People are still swayed by its most sincere form. A young friend of mine admits that although she doesn't count on a date to hold the door, plan a special dinner, or bring flowers as a surprise, that doesn't stop her from hoping she will find a man who will do such romantic things and more.

> **MAMA'S MOJO** Share some romantic experiences with your kids. Tell the good stories—I know you have at least one. Rent a fun, romantic movie and watch it together. Listen to some love songs without the "F" word. Talk up romance; make it come alive and create an expectation for its possibilities in your teenager's life.

Hold Out for Moonlight and Reality

Romance can be overdramatized on TV and in many popular novels. It's important that your kids know the difference between soap opera romance and the real thing. Help them understand that real life is not all about constant swooning, trips around the world, or endless parties. Such things aren't realistic for regular working people—especially when the children arrive. Teach them the tricks to keeping romance strong while they work, raise children, and clean their house. After all, few people can stay home and be wooed all day long. Who is going to pay the light bill? Hey, couples can still make out in the kitchen while the kids are busy, or flirt until they go to sleep. Remind your children to look for someone who will do that, because—once again—most of a couple's life together goes on outside the bedroom, not in it.

> **MAMA'S MOJO** Can't stand the girl or guy your child is seeing because you know he or she is wrong, wrong, wrong? Listen, don't say too much. If you do, that poor-choice love object will become ten times more appealing. It's true, so here's your plan: train your kids well enough so that person will get on their nerves for the same reasons you don't like him or her. That way, your child will probably dump the "offender" without you having to lift a finger.

Don't push the "good ones" too hard, either. Just stand back and hope they'll stick with them because you have already helped them see what's good.

If a mama praises and pushes a girl on her son too strongly, he will always find a reason not to date her. The same thing goes for a guy. I know because Kenny was that guy—the one who made mothers roll out the red carpet. Although I was proud of his reputation, girls didn't want to date him because their mamas talked him up so much.

The Search for a Soul Mate
Is Meant to Be

I have often told my children how their father was such a true love in my life. I was blessed to have married my friend, my confidante, and my lover. He was the person who completed me. I believe in fate like the Jewish concept of *B'shert*, which translates as "meant to be." I want my kids to settle for nothing less than whoever was "meant to be" the love of their life—the right soul mate who will cherish them and whom they can treasure. That's my dearest wish.

It is our responsibility to make our children aware of our values about sex and romance. They may not choose our values, but we have to share what is important to us.

During my first night alone with Julius, I remember rose petals in the bathwater and a shared bottle of champagne. What a different experience that was than if a girl's boyfriend comes over, the blanket is on the floor—and that's it. When sex is only recreation there can't be a depth of feeling. Where is the love? Where is the tenderness? By sharing what you have experienced—or what you know is possible—you can teach your kids how to look for the potential of a full, loving relationship before they jump into a merely sexual one.

The Kissing Connection

Remember that big hit "The Shoop Shoop Song (It's in His Kiss)" by Rudy Clark? Everybody recorded it. I think Cher, Lulu, Aretha Franklin, and even Linda Ronstadt produced a version. Remember the lyrics?—"If you want to know if he loves you so . . . it's in his kiss." Think about that for a while. It's powerfully true.

One of my favorite movies is *Pretty Woman* because the Julia Roberts character was so much more than just a prostitute. One time my foster daughter and I were watching that movie. She asked me why prostitutes don't kiss. I answered her: a kiss is such an important part of romance, we can't forget how intimate it can be.

Have you seen those dating shows where people are tongue kissing when they just met an hour ago? What? Who starts tongue kissing right away? Maybe it's a generational thing. Listen, Julius kissed me on the cheek for such a long time I was afraid maybe he was gay or something. I finally shouted at him one night (after he'd planted one on my *forehead*), "Wait a damn minute. What's going on here? We are dating for a month, and we are still kissing on the forehead?" He smiled and whispered how much he already cared and that was why he was taking it slowly. Oh, he was smooth.

Don't get me wrong; no one is a tease if she kisses someone special with real passion. It's not a green light for going all the way. A real kiss means a lot all by itself.

Don't Stand for a One-Night Stand

What about those one-night stands? No matter how we women want to pretend it doesn't matter, it does matter—of course it does! Help your child set standards (and help her understand double standards) so she won't turn into a statistic. Remind your daughters how bad they will feel if he doesn't call the next day, or worse, if he never calls them again. I don't care what they say now, it hurts when it happens. It hurts even more if they are left with a souvenir like pregnancy or a serious medical problem—nothing is 100 percent foolproof. I impressed on my daughter Andi to believe in true love so she wouldn't let down her guard or jeopardize her life for someone who might never call her back. I told her to set standards so she wouldn't turn into a statistic.

It woke me up to the lack of self-respect in some girls today when I recently watched a Maury show on TV. It featured a pregnant girl who had slept with at least twenty men in the not-so-distant past. Surprise! She didn't have a clue about who might be her baby's daddy. That's an extreme example of a subculture, but it *is* a subculture, I hate to say it. That culture doesn't have strong values or even a basic sense of respect, but I can't blame the girls. They just don't understand it. They've never been taught what it is to have self-respect.

Never once did anyone on this show offer one bit of constructive advice to this messed-up guest—I couldn't believe it. And what about the audience? What kind of message would they walk away with from the show? Why can't some advice be offered for viewers who might be on the same dead-end road as one of the guests? Well, I've got something to say about that!

Even if a TV show with a troubled guest doesn't offer any helpful advice, a parent sure can dish it out. When you watch the show with your kids, talk about why you think that pregnant girl needs counseling. Bring up her apparent absence of birth control. Ask your kids what they think of her and her future child's chances in this world. If you can do that, these shows can serve as good teachable moments—grab them and go to town. If the kids didn't see a certain show like that, bring it up and make the same points by asking your kids similar questions.

Underneath it all, I feel sorry for young girls like the pregnant girl on Maury's show. I get angry or disgusted, but I can't stay that way. Remember Rizzo in the movie *Grease*? There's always a girl like Rizzo. Usually underneath all her promiscuity is a cry for something deeper—a longing for real love.

I was pleased my daughter Andi felt confident enough to tell me when a fellow had invited her to visit him in another city. I told her so.

"You really trust him?" she asked me in a most disbelieving tone.

"No, I trust you," I said. "You're mature and we've already talked. But whatever you do, you are going to do what's right for you." I also told her if he didn't try to run her around the apartment, she would have something to worry about!

> MAMA'S MOJO Sometimes you just have to be seen
> as a woman, not just a mother. You need to switch from
> mother-daughter dialogue to woman-to-woman. As a

mother you have told them what they need. There are times
to relate to your older girls as a woman. Boys need to
see you as a woman too. They will treat other women
differently if they realize their mother is a woman. ⌋

The Curse of the Weekend Woman

I don't want my daughter to live with a guy. I don't even want her
to be his "weekend woman." If she was a guy's "W-word," I really
don't want to know. By the same token, I know my sons have
spent weekends with women. I also know that they were not interested in them other than spending the weekend. Because I
know this, I don't want my daughters to be one of them.

Ever listen to Betty Wright? She's a great soul and R&B
singer—and a strong influence in the hip-hop world. Her lyrics
nail down some of the sexual pitfalls for women.

"U-R-A-Ho and U Don't Know" *by Betty Wright*

How will you ever find a love that's true?
Letting every man do what he wants to do to you . . .

Sing it, Betty! This is where women make the *big mistake.* They
don't hold out. It hurts to find out the man they slept with every
weekend took another girl to meet his parents. It's an amazing
thing with us mamas; we still understand that boys know there are
girls they don't bring home. These girls serve a different purpose.
It is a hard thing for a woman to say, but the double standard still

exists today. There are girls who are there for the experience (that would be sex, ladies). This has never changed. The man moves on to someone else and those types of girls are left behind.

Boys may want to date the fast girls, but they don't bring them home for their mama's scrutiny. It's just something you don't do. Girls also like bad boys—especially the tough guys, the classic James Dean types. Many girls keep their bad boy a secret—they wouldn't dare bring him home.

> **MAMA MOJO** Tried and true boyfriend mojo: watch how a man treats his mother. He'll probably treat a girlfriend or wife the same way sooner or later.

Live Up to a Good Reputation

A bad reputation is hard to live down. Don't let your kids get run over by a fast girl or bad boy. Your child's good reputation can be one of his or her most important assets.

There was an episode on my son Chris's TV show, *Everybody Hates Chris*, about reputations. The main character—known as Chris—came over to his next-door neighbor girl's house to help her catch a loose mouse. He caught it for her. Out of gratitude, the young girl kissed him on his way out the door. Some of the nosey neighborhood folks (yep, you know the type)

Kenny: I've hung around fast women. They don't intrigue me anymore. If they are Lamborghini fast—whew, watch out! Even classic Mercedes fast can get you into trouble. Fast women have bigger bad consequences than the average girl—so beware.

Tony: Andre and Chrissy would always say to me: "Tone, you are too picky to be a 'player.'" I would party—I know a zillion girls—but, at the end of the day, it is only a small, select group whom I could consider in any serious way.

saw that kiss. Word spread. Older girls gave Chris their phone number and boys gave him winks. You know how it is. Chris liked the attention so much, he let those assumptions ride. Finally, the girl's grandmother heard the gossip and angrily reported her findings to Chris's TV family. He ended up being pressured to go around and tell everyone in the neighborhood that "nothing happened" to save her reputation. Of course, his reputation as a teenage "player" was nipped in the bud.

Be a Full-Course Meal—Not a Sexy Snack

Every mother would like to believe in her heart of hearts that her daughter is a virgin. In these times, that may not be realistic. There are kids who are into abstinence, who have decided to wait for sexual involvement. It's not only about "just say no." It's about a value system. It comes down to a parent's ability to teach moral values that fortify teenagers so they can wait and understand what is important and when the time is right.

Tell your daughters, if their dates want a "snack," why not suggest they go to McDonald's. As a parent of teenage daughters, one of the things I taught my girls was to have a strong sense of self-worth. If a guy is not ready for my daughter as a full-course, meaningful relationship—fine. However, she doesn't need to provide him with any hors d'oeuvres—you know what I'm talking about!

A mama needs to be strong and keep the lines of communication open. Teach your girls to be "princesses." Show them how to be respected for their own special selves. My daughter Andi jokes about not being a princess, but she says, "If the crown happens to fit me, what can I do but put it on?" Believe me, it fits quite well on my Andi.

Some things never change. Guys still say dramatically, "If you loved me, you would . . ." Hey, what about you, girl? This is the hardest lesson. It's about loving yourself so you don't need anyone else's approval. Having sex is one of the biggest steps you can take in life. The right time is when it is right for you in every way—not because it's good for someone else.

> **MAMA'S MOJO** Offer a sexual "first time checklist"
> for your child to consider. Have him or her answer just
> three questions: 1. Are you both in love—really in love?
> 2. Where is this relationship going—or not going? 3. Who is
> responsible for protection—and what will you use? Bottom
> line: if your child cannot discuss these things or act on
> them with a partner, neither one is responsible enough
> for having sex. Period.

Because I Said So—and I Did So

I love to tell this story about the time Julius and I went to a social event. We sat together, and whispered and laughed all evening. Later, someone asked me about the identity of my hot date.

She couldn't believe it was my husband because—according to her—married people have nothing to talk or laugh about.

Role models do matter. In our Rock household, there was a world of love and laughs. Even though Julius and I were the parents, we had a separate, deep relationship with each other. Our children were blessed to be able to watch us have good times together. It was a model for them to follow when the time came for them to settle down with one person.

Andre: My brothers and I wanted someone who acted like our mama did at home. We liked the way she treated Daddy with respect—and didn't ever wear hair rollers when he was around.

The boys always talked about how I tried to look good whenever Daddy was around. You know what? He did the same thing. The minute he got home, he'd change downstairs from his work clothes into something nice. Only then would he come upstairs and give me a hello kiss. He always looked great.

Let your kids know how you grew up, especially when it comes to your relationships with the opposite sex. Now if you were a slut or a bad boy, you should definitely tone it down for the kids. However, everyone can share some memories like prom night, a first kiss, real love, and other such experiences.

I adored my father and he adored me. I had a picture in my mind of what I looked for in a man because of him. My daddy, Wesley James Tingman, was an upright man and a hard worker in everything he did. He even built our family house, which is still standing in Andrews, South Carolina. He was strong, but he was kind and loving too. That's what I wanted—a solid, decent man with a gentle heart. Thank God, I found my Julius and was able to live with him as long as I did. If you are widowed, as I was, it is important to talk about your late spouse and the good memories. My grandchildren were born after Julius passed away. We tell stories about him and show family snapshots. We keep his memory alive and fresh. When they pass a picture of him in the hallway of my house, they yell out, "That's my Grandpa!"

We always talked about times like that. My kids still like to hear about my first date with Julius, especially the part when I tell them I didn't like him at first, and then, when we finally went out and we talked nonstop. I knew that night I was going to marry him. He didn't know until much later.

You can laugh together about the differences between dating in the sixties or seventies and today. Back then, there were people in town who knew you wherever you went. Parent chaperones were a fixture at major functions. You didn't just go out "somewhere"—you had to have a specific place to go, like the local diner or the Attic Nightclub in Myrtle Beach.

Tony: If I'm going out with someone, I always ask if her parents are still together. If they are not, I want to make sure she won't walk away if things get tough. When you make a commitment to somebody, you don't fight the same way. You don't run away from problems— you try to work it out. That's what I want!

If you are separated or divorced, point out healthy relationships around you. Don't dwell on the negative part of your last relationship—it's tough, but *don't do it*! If your "ex" spends any time with the children—hallelujah! Let the kids experience that parent fully and draw their own conclusions. They usually do, I promise.

So what if your family is more Ozzy and Sharon than Ozzie and

Harriet? Kids learn to be responsible adults by seeing good role models. Make it your business to find those adults among friends, teachers, or members of the congregation where you worship. Borrow them to spend time with your family.

Our youngest son, Jordan, spends time with his best friend's parents. They have a great relationship. Boys who don't have fathers need to see strong, positive men who can relate well to women.

Whenever you allow your child to see adults care and respect each other, you give them the best chance to fully love and be loved. In the end, that's what you want as a parent, don't you?

OK, fast pep-talk review: sex education is not a backstage pass to have sex. Take charge by having *The Talk* and answering questions honestly—don't leave it to your child's friends or siblings to get to them first. Help your kids to wise up so they don't end up living with something or someone that could cramp their style, health, and reputation for a lifetime.

And, of course, don't talk about sex without talking about responsibility and relationships—it's too beautiful, personal, and blessed to simply be a recreational sport. Sex is meant to be between people who love and care about each other and for the children they create.

Now look, if you haven't given *The Talk* by now, or even tried, what are you waiting for? Take a deep breath. Blow it out slowly—you can do it.

Remember Mama Rock's Rules and Strategies

- **Parents Know Best**

  Parents must take charge of sex education. A mom or dad can give The Talk *to both boys and girls. Don't leave the job to friends or siblings if you want to get it right.*

- **Don't Just Talk About Sex, Talk About Responsibility and Relationships**

  Sex is not just a recreational sport; it's meant to be between people who love and care for each other and for the children they create.

- **Don't Worry About "Tell and Do"**

  Sex education is not a backstage pass for having sex. Take care and take charge by answering questions honestly and getting real with your children about protection.

- **Don't Lie Down with Anything You Don't Want to Live with Forever**

  Wise up your kids so they don't end up living with someone who cramps their style, their health, and their reputation all their life—not for boys only!

- **You Can't Wear a Paternity Suit**

  "Who is your daddy?" can be the question of a lifetime. Be aware of the tangle of responsibility and consequence when you bring a child into the world outside of marriage.

- Take the "F" out of Romance

    Some may say romance is dead; help your child understand it is possible and worth waiting for.

- Hold Out for Moonlight and Reality

    It's hard to believe in fairy tales. Believe anyway and don't settle—be on the lookout for your soul mate.

- Don't Stand for a One-Night Stand

    Is your child a "ho" and she just doesn't know? Tell her not to jeopardize her life for someone who might never call back.

- Because I Said So and Did So

    It's critical to understand the importance of role models—and how to find them—especially if your family is more Ozzy and Sharon Osbourne than Ozzie and Harriet Nelson.

Good Memories Are the Best Things You Can Give Your Children (Besides Good Manners)

GOOD MEMORIES ARE PRECIOUS. They can sustain and inspire us.

I never understood the true importance of good memories until Julius died. I was grief-stricken and didn't want to do anything. My sister-in-law, Elaine, urged me to remember the fun times Julius and I had together—she said to be grateful for the wonderful memories I did have. She was right, it was the memories of our life together that kept me going. It seemed when I was at my lowest someone would tell me a great "Buster" story (Buster was Julius's nickname), and the laughter we shared about those stories would buoy my spirit. As we recounted those happy times, it gave me hope that life would be good once again.

I continue to be supported by the memories of our family life together. When I listen to my children tell the stories of their lives, I'm often moved to tears when I realize Julius and I helped make some of those good memories possible. My fondest hope is that our children will always try to give their children positive, inspirational, and often hilarious things to remember. And I pray all of us will have more time together to create new memories, traditions, and fun in the years to come.

Share "Before You Were Born" Memories

Children love to hear how much they were loved, even before they were born. They like to hear the crazy details of what happened in your rush to the hospital or all the happy things that went on when you were carrying them—they really do. Be sure to talk up the days before each child was born as often as you can when a newer arrival—another baby—is on the way.

Brian never tires of the story of how he was born in our car across the street from White Castle. That day, before I left the house, I wanted to put out the children's cereal bowls and write a short note in each one. Julius kept on urging me to leave. Well, finally I left—a little too late to make it to the hospital—and Brian had his first car ride moments after his arrival.

Don't be afraid to tell your child you are pregnant because of what he might say. Before Brian was born, Tony was not ready to give up his role as the baby in the family. I'll never forget when he said, "When that baby gets out of your stomach and comes home, I'm going to slap him." The first chance he got, he tried to do it, too. When it came time for Andi's birth, he said, "I don't want no baby girl." After she was born, though, he treated her like a little doll. Now he vies with Brian in a friendly rivalry over who is closer to Andi. So, let your children know a new baby is on the way. It will help them to share in the preparation and excitement.

> **MAMA'S MOJO** Be sure to explain right away to your youngest ones about the changes they will see in you—so they aren't scared of your ballooning tummy. Tell them you remember when they were in the same tummy and how you loved them before you saw them.

Lay on the love all around when you tell your children about their new brother or sister. From the youngest to the oldest, the message is the same: each child will be an important part in the new baby's life, and Mama has enough love for everyone (because you do, mamas). Also, don't tell him things will remain just the same (because they won't)! Talk up the wonderful days before each child was born. Keep it up even more in connection with the last days of your pregnancy before the newest arrival is in the house.

The children loved to hear my memories about the times I was expecting. I'd tell them about our maternity shopping day. Julius and I would wait until my tummy grew round. Then, we'd plan a shopping day at Lady Madonna maternity shop on Avenue M and Nostrand Avenue in Brooklyn. Julius would take a seat in one of their green wicker chairs. We'd spend the afternoon while I tried on different outfits and paraded by his chair in a personal fashion show. He'd say those magic words: "Buy anything you want!" He made me feel beautiful and fashionable—not the first things that come to mind—during those times.

Get Away from It All—With Your Family

I wanted my children's memories of their childhood to be happy ones as much as possible. They caught fireflies and biked all day when we went to Long Island in the summer. When we'd come back home to Brooklyn, the sprinklers would be turned on and all the neighborhood kids would gather to run through them until dusk. I still smile about the times we'd all go on family vacations to Pennsylvania. We'd double up in Econo Lodge rooms and explore all the amusement parks in the state, including Hershey Park. It was always a great adventure. We even snuck in some school shopping at the outlets in Reading, Pennsylvania.

Family vacations are wonderful memory makers and meaningful experiences for a family because there is nothing in the way of being together. Whatever your budget allows, take the time—even if it's just a few days—to make lifetime memories with your whole crew.

Know Your Family by Your Traditions

Family traditions help to make the various members of your clan become a "we." The core values and beliefs and—hopefully—a sense of humor are discovered in traditions. I know our family continues to stay strong when traditions and memories are handed down—it is our own personal history, from what we serve at holidays to always giving the children new books at Christmas to helping others in the neighborhood. There is a sense of security, character, and emotional closeness from a family life rich in traditions large and small, silly and serious. All of this reinforces a positive outlook for a child and is a source of strength and comfort for an adult.

Although family traditions are not limited to holidays, most of them seem to be involved with the holidays because they are so important and because the extended family gathers together at those times. There are also, though, smaller, everyday traditions you may not think about that can create a part of your family's identity and be a great source of memories. For instance, the way my kids waited for their chance to go call Daddy for dinner; or what about when you go to that certain place for a treat every time you shop nearby; or the indoor picnics you have when the weather turns bleak. It can even be when your kids help you cook at certain meals. Julius created a beautiful tradition with the birth of each of our children. He would always give me a special gift in honor of each new baby. He said I'd given him the greatest gift ever—a new child. I soon realized that I had, because our children are truly an expression of our life everlasting. We live through our children and our grandchildren—and through our traditions and memories. Celebrate the old memories and create new ones whenever you can.

Keep On "Keeping On"

I married the oldest son of the Rock family. When his mother passed away, it was up to us to keep on doing the same things she would have wanted at holiday time. In the same way that Julius and I kept up his mother's holiday traditions, I believe that Chris and his wife Malaak, and Andre and his wife Sandy will step up and try to do certain traditions just like their father and I did.

It is also valuable for every one of my children to create their own traditions. Sometimes Malaak will serve something special for dinner when Andi comes for a visit. She will say, "It's your mother's classic recipe." It is, but she'll put a little spin on it with her own touch. That's great! That's the way it should be.

There is definitely a balancing act between old family traditions and what you want to create within your own family. Once Julius and I got married and created our own family unit, both sets of parents and all the siblings turned into extended family.

Despite our large and extended families, some things were just "ours." We became a "we" with our own traditions. I was selfish with my children that way, but not in a bad sense. There were holiday happenings that were just for our immediate family. Of course, we included and were included in other traditions, but I wanted us to have our own separate ones, too.

Do what feels right for you and what you have established with your family—and get ready to compromise. Don't change your own, newer traditions just because Grandma came for the holidays. If you want to honor her with one of her old favorites, go right ahead. If you don't care for turkey on Christmas but your mother insists on it, serve a turkey along with whatever you had planned. Come on, be flexible. Don't just say: "This is what my mama did for the holidays so that's what we *have* to do in our house." You can figure out a way to make it all work.

Narrow the Generation Gap with Family Traditions

Ann: I remember fondly the holidays at home when Mama Rock would make a big Southern dinner—after all, she was a Southern girl just like me—with turkey, chicken, meat, collard greens, macaroni and cheese, cornbread stuffing, and her unbelievable biscuits and her legendary Sweet Potato Pie—*I loved that pie! All of us did, including Julius, who liked it almost as much as his favorite dish: steak and gravy with onions and a big dollop of Worcestershire sauce on top. He'd always say "pass the* 'what's-this-here sauce.'" *It became a family tradition for us to say the same thing. I think of him whenever I see a bottle of Worcestershire sauce.*

Christmas was a big deal in our families. My early married life with the Rock family was exciting. It was traditional for us to dress up for Christmas dinner at the Rocks. My sisters-in-law were all fashion plates and loved outdoing each other in the fashion department. There were fourteen siblings and their respective spouses, girlfriends, boyfriends, children, cousins—well, you can imagine. Everyone of all ages joined in at that big family dinner where Grandma Mary Rock would outshine herself with one of her huge, delicious feasts.

At our house, everybody joined in to bake chocolate chip cookies for Santa on Christmas Eve. They were the kids' favorite, so I guess they were Santa's pick, too. This year Andi baked with her nieces Lola and Zarah (they made alphabet cookies instead of chocolate chip).

Holiday preparation time offers an opportunity to include all the generations. Even the youngest can help with cookies, candies, breads, or cakes. The little ones can stir the bowl, pour in the milk—and even a baby can lick the frosting! This also goes for other traditions like stringing popcorn—the younger ones can hand the popcorn kernels from a bowl to the "stringer"—you get the idea. Get everyone involved.

The fun part is what attracts the children to an activity. Did you play with Tinkertoys, Pick-up sticks, or other classic toys or board games? Get them for your kids and show them how it is done—keep that tradition going. Choose something all ages can play. Share the stories about what you did with those toys or games when you were a kid—include whom you played with and all that. You are establishing a connection with the generations—besides, parents, you might have forgotten how much you loved those games. Anyway, sometimes your kids can't believe you were ever young—so remind them as you finish constructing a Mr. Potato Head in record time.

Follow the Pajama Principle

The most meaningful traditions provide a sense of security and a feeling of belonging. That doesn't mean they have to be serious or stuffy. Some traditions are hard to drop. I thought that after my kids grew up they wouldn't care about the new pajamas I always gave as gifts on Christmas. Was I ever wrong! One time, Tony didn't see his new pajamas and was upset until he found them. There was something about all of us receiving new PJs and wearing them on Christmas that created the safe, secure feeling that as long as we had those new pajamas our world would be all right—no matter what. That is the Pajama Principle—a tradition that makes you feel the way our pajamas made us feel is a definite keeper.

Andre: It wouldn't be Christmas without new pajamas—it just wouldn't. I guess it wouldn't seem like it either if my mother, to this day, did not still put those little Matchbox cars inside our Christmas stockings.

Good Memories Don't Have to Cost Good Money

When I was young, my dad worked away from home as a construction worker. He usually had to go away to make decent wages. Friday would be the day Daddy came home each week. We were all excited. You know, he never came home without something for us children—even if it hadn't been a particularly good week for him. We didn't care if it was just some candy, it was the fact that he remembered us.

Among the holiday memories I treasure from childhood was when my dad would decorate the ceilings with crepe paper and those little crepe paper balls for the holidays. We may not have had lots of money, but my parents knew how to celebrate, and they passed that ability down to me. Celebrating anything isn't all about money, it is about the joy of any holiday or special occasion. It is about wanting to honor it, to do something special to make it meaningful to your family and a tradition to remember.

Christmas in my Andrews, South Carolina, childhood days was a neighborhood affair. It was a high-spirited season without a high price tag. The streets would be full of kids dashing from house to house. We don't see that anymore. All of us would share the joy if one of our friends got something special—if someone got a bike, everyone took turns and rode the day away. Back then, people started baking cakes in November. Lord, every house had an abundance of sweets. My brothers and I would go house to house and get a handful of nuts at this house or an orange at that one and always something sweet and delicious to eat. For us, that was what Christmas was all about. We may have wanted things we didn't get, but we understood the circumstances and relished the spirit of the day. Those memories are as sweet now as my favorite treat from those days—a piece of rich Christmas pound cake.

Today, an excellent idea would be a "Light Night" family outing. Round up everyone (if there are many family members, form a car caravan) and head out to see holiday lights around the neighborhood, in the city, or at a special display. We used to go out on Long Island to see the holiday lights. Another idea is to take the children on "Artwalks" (which goes on at any season, not just Christmas), when a group of shops and galleries hosts an open house for looking at art, shopping, and sharing some refreshments. Just going ice skating and having hot chocolate afterward is a special time. There are so many things to do as a family to create memories that cost little and last a lifetime.

At Christmas, one of our simplest, cheapest, and best traditions was when we all watched a movie classic on TV together. Remember, those were the days before VCRs, TiVo, or rental movies by mail. A favorite classic came on TV during its scheduled time and we watched it right then for however long it would take—no pause or rewind button was available. Tony and Andre loved *A Christmas Story* and got Jordan hooked on it too. The funniest part is when the movies would begin on TV, the kids would call me to come in from the kitchen: "Mommy, Mommy, hurry up, the movie started." They'd act like something was going to happen in the movie that I'd never seen before.

Brian: Simple things stick out in a child's mind like our favorite traditional Christmas breakfast. On the table were steaming bowls of oatmeal, Pop-Tarts, and a cup of hot chocolate rich with marshmallows. I still remember it like yesterday—the anticipation, the joy of being with our family and celebrating with our traditions. I remember those things more than some expensive gift or another.

You don't need to go all over the place or spend a fortune to find family activities that create great memories. Have a "Board Game Dinner Night"—we still do that. Pick out a board game and play it with your children or ask another family to join you. Don't feel the need to prepare a big meal; just put something on the grill. Those times end up being so much fun and it encourages kids today to think about playing board games instead of video games.

I liked the happy weekends on our block in Brooklyn. Like many families everywhere, we had a station wagon—a Country Squire. Saturday would be our family day. We'd load up the kids and go shopping or do whatever we had to do as a team. Even though much of what we were doing involved errands, it seemed like such a grand time because we made it that way. We remember those Saturdays as an important part of our family culture.

One of our favorite Easter traditions is simple: we include little, inexpensive personal gifts inside our Easter baskets along with the candy and eggs. When my boys were young, I'd slip a Matchbox car into the basket. Last year, I put some bath oil in Andi's basket (yes, I still give my adult children Easter baskets). Malaak is always on the lookout for little trinkets to put in the baskets for her girls. Although we traditionally put Cadbury Cream Eggs in the baskets, nobody really likes them except Tony—so he scores! We all look forward to sorting out the goodies and making candy trades with each. It's a great tradition at little cost.

Don't Make Stress a Holiday Tradition

Try not to make holidays a tradition of stress—especially Christmas or Hanukkah. A holiday tradition should not be "we always spend too much and have post-holiday anxiety until next July." One of my strong memories is how Julius always said that by December

26th, everybody knew Christmas was coming again next year. He'd say that to his friends who spoke of their big bills at Christmas. After all, there was a whole year to plan before it happened. He started to put money away for the following year. He was right about how important it is not to anticipate the holidays with financial dread or have your holiday memories reduced each month to a giant credit card bill.

Something Julius said before he died was that he would always be there. One November day, he was, even though we had already lost him. I was worried about financial things because he died without an executor. Andre was in college, Brian and Kenny in private schools. I didn't know how we could celebrate the holiday season just around the corner. I went to the mail. Inside was a huge insurance check from John Hancock. It was so typical of Julius that he took care of everything right on time. I stood in the vestibule just staring at the check. I told Brian, and we went out to do some Christmas shopping. When we got back, Brian stepped into his Dad's role and hid all the things for everyone, just like Julius used to do long before the actual holiday—it was such a comfort that he followed that custom.

Keep That "Junk"—It Could Be an Heirloom

It's folk wisdom: one person's junk is another person's treasure. Family heirlooms are always important memories no matter what. I am not only referring to valuable antiques, art, or jewelry.

I also include those items that matter to you and your children. For example, your wedding or christening gowns, certain dolls—like the one Tony made me when he was in the fourth grade—or that string and macaroni bracelet your second-grader made for your birthday.

When you frame a handwritten note or drawing from your child, you have instantly created a keepsake. It takes on more meaning as the child gets older and may become a passed-down treasure. I framed a card Jordan gave me when he was eight years old; it features a hand-drawn self-portrait and a poem about my kitchen—it is still hanging on the wall of the kitchen even though he's now a teenager. It means so much to both of us. Someday, I'd like to imagine Jordan hanging that in his house for his children to see.

Christmas ornaments are perfect for heirlooms. Every ornament my kids ever made in school is on our Christmas tree. "Where's my ornament?" is a big question when the kids come back home year after year. Even though they try to act nonchalant, I know they love it. Each year as I bring them out we are filled with happy nostalgia and loads of stories.

I kept a lock of hair from each of my children. They love that I kept it along with the tiny hospital bracelet they wore on their arms when I brought them home as new babies. We would marvel together at the bracelets and how they could ever have been that little.

For children, home is wherever their mother or father is. It is especially true when children have lost or moved from their childhood home (like we did from Decatur Street to South Carolina). So bring with you as many of those "heirlooms" for every child and all the pictures and journals you can to make your children a home wherever you are.

Treasure Your Memories in an Oral History

As far as family "heirlooms," it is important to remember not only the objects of the past, but also the stories of those living who remember the past. That is called an oral history. During the holidays when families get together is a great time to have your family members record those tales (especially the older relatives) on tape or in a journal memory book. So many families leave all the storytelling to "Aunt Edna," and then when she is gone, no one knows the stories. This way you can protect those memories and they will be a treasure forever, and I do mean forever.

MAMA'S MOJO Don't limit the oral history to the impressive or "positive" stories only. Every family has bad memories or a time when someone didn't live up to their potential and everyone was worried about them. Sharing those tales and talking about what happened can serve as a good example and help others learn to do better. Older family members should seek out the younger ones and include them as they write or record their stories. It is a bonding experience and it can be inspiring—especially if the younger relatives ask questions. Who knows what might be discovered?

Remember: There's Always Something to Be Thankful For

During my childhood we did not celebrate Thanksgiving, maybe because we could not afford to. After I got married, we went to my mother-in-law's house and had a big family dinner. Later, as my family grew, we'd celebrate Thanksgiving at home. I always remember our big house full of people, stories, music, and cutting up. There would be football games after dinner and the kids would go outside for a pickup football game.

We always held hands during dinner while we spoke about what each of us was thankful for. Kenny, who was in elementary school, listened closely to the grateful words. At his turn, he sincerely said what he was thankful for: *Teenage Mutant Ninja Turtles.*

All holidays and special days hold an element of thankfulness. It is important to learn what makes a family member happy, and it is even more important to learn what he or she is grateful for and why. The spirit of appreciation should run through all you do as a family—never mind what it is you appreciate at the time.

My children, through the years, did so many sweet things to let me know how much they appreciated and loved me. One of my biggest surprises was when Chris gifted me with a little Miata convertible. It was outside my house one day tied up in a big bow. When I called to thank him I was crying. He started crying, too, and said, "Don't thank me, Mommy, I'm thanking you."

Keep Santa and the Tooth Fairy
for as Long as You Can

Kids are kids for such a short time. Fantasy and the belief in the unknown is a part of childhood and gives us some of our most beloved memories and traditions. What child hasn't put his tooth under a pillow and waited for the tooth fairy? Hey, even after he decides maybe—just maybe—there isn't a tooth fairy, doesn't he still put his tooth under the pillow (in case) and look for money?

I never told my kids there was no Santa, or Easter Bunny, Tooth Fairy, or other favorites—I still haven't. They were as real for them as the sun and the moon. Every culture has its whimsical characters and spirits. I think it takes childhood away to tell your kids to stop believing at a certain age. After all, I think as long as there are parents and children, Santa and all the magical traditions still exist without age limit—at least in our hearts.

Andi told me she would always believe in Santa Claus. After all, she says, I might as well buy a gift and hand it to her if we didn't do the Santa tradition. She and Jordan can't wait to go to sleep on Christmas Eve so they can get up in the morning and see what Santa gave them.

We continue the tradition of "Santa's footprints" in our house. How is that possible? (*Warning: Don't read this, Lola—skip to the next paragraph.*) The secret is out: we take a pair of the biggest shoes we can find (they used to be Julius's, but now they are Jordan's shoes), dip the soles in white flour, and walk up and back in them from the fireplace to the tree. You see, those big white footprints are Santa's footprints. They seem like they were made from the snow on his boots, but the white stuff never melts. It's great! I'm so glad he still "visits" everyone in our family no matter where we are during the holidays.

Share the Greatness of Grandparents

Attention Grandparents: One great part of being a grandparent is that you CAN be friends with your grandchild—you don't have to choose between being a grandparent and a friend. The thing is, you need to respect the rules your kids (as parents) have laid down for your grandchildren. Now, I know you will buy the stuff parents won't buy and you will let your grandchildren eat what their parents won't let them indulge in—my father did that—but, hey, that's a grandparent's right within limits.

Grandparents have so much to give, to teach, and so many memories to share with your children in ways you may not even imagine. My boys and their buddy, Randy Richardson, will never forget those trips to South Carolina to see my parents. Julius and I would stay for a week and then let the boys stay with my family. We'd return later in the summer to pick them up, so they got a chance to really spend some time. Summers or long vacation breaks are a good time to have your children spend time with their grandparents if they don't live close by, especially if you can leave them to bond without you being right there.

By the time the boys started their summer visits to Andrews, South Carolina, my father, Wesley Tingman, had retired and opened a small store on Main Street. The sign out front of his place said "Tingman Snack Bar." One of the best features of summer, the kids told me, was to go down to the store where my dad would let them sample boiled peanuts, candy, and other treats—see what I told you, my dad would let them have all kinds of goodies. My kids, who grew up in Brooklyn where they couldn't ride bikes in the street, won't ever forget how they could ride their bikes all over the town of Andrews.

MAMA'S MOJO Encourage your parents to tell their grandchildren about the "old days and times." Have them tell the stories and show pictures or souvenirs from places they have been or things they have done. Be sure to tell them to tell it all—again, not just the good things. Your children also love to hear about what you did when you were little (but tell them to go easy on you when they talk to your kids).

The greatest gift for my children, in many ways, was when some local residents would come up to my boys and say, "Aren't you Wesley Tingman's 'grands'?" When the boys answered yes, there would be smiles all around and pats on the back. My dad was respected in Andrews—which was a good thing for them to see—but there was something else: those boys behaved all summer because everybody knew who they were (and whose they were). They were related!

My boys were blessed with the chance to know Grandpa Wesley and Grandma Pearl Tingman and Grandpa (Reverend) Allen and Grandma Mary Rock. They also knew their Great-Grandmother

Brian: I remember Grandma Pearl as one of the most beautiful women I ever met in my life. She had a calm, soft-spoken demeanor, and a humility about everything she did. Who could forget her Southern-style breakfasts? There was no box of cereal for us—no way—we are talking a full meal of grits, eggs, sausages, bacon, toast, and OJ. Whenever we woke up, it was there in the kitchen ready for us—that was her way.

Emma Tingman. Chris, as the oldest, was even blessed to know his Great-Grandmother Maggie McClam. Even though they are all gone now, the boys can remember their love, the good times, and the traditions. All those memories and the influence of their grandparents and great-grandparents are theirs to keep and draw from when they need to feel good or strong.

Anytime your child can create good memories with a grandparent adds to the richness of his life. It also teaches about continuity and the tradition of generations. Make the time to get your children and their grandparents together any way you can.

MAMA'S MOJO Try some *mail mojo*. If a grandparent lives far away, start early and have your children write letters and share pictures with their grandparents via the U.S. Mail. Your little girl can dictate a letter to you for Grandma if she can't write. Let your son decorate the letter with crayon "creations." Yes, you can use e-mail, but be sure to use hard copy as much as you can (or copy your e-mails if you must)—it lasts longer and that collection of correspondence can be reread and passed on for years to come—just like I read my grandmother's correspondence after she had passed away. And nothing beats the rush of a real letter in the mailbox addressed to your child from his grandparents.

It's Never Too Late for Traditions

Maybe you say you don't have any traditions—or not enough to keep your family connected. Once again, don't be so sure. Traditions aren't written in stone. Sometimes they just happen. Maybe every year all of you go to Aunt Sadie's house and then on the way back you always stop for a sundae at the one place that's open on Christmas—there it is—that's one for you. Maybe it's just a certain bedtime ritual that you always do—or would like to do. See how easy it is?

My mother-in-law, Mary, had a little tradition between the two of us. She was not a coffee drinker like me, but she kept a little jar of instant coffee and she would prepare it every time I came over to visit. She was the only person I knew who boiled instant coffee in a pot on the stove. Oh, but it was a good cup of coffee, let me tell you. The fact that she did it for me was so special.

> MAMA'S MOJO Doing something for others is always a good tradition to start at any holiday. Try Christmas caroling as a group or bring some of your homemade baked goods to a nursing home—and stay awhile. If you know of someone who needs help at the season (relative, neighbor, or friend), now is the time to set up that tradition, whether it's a "help clean up day" or "cook a meal for him or her," or whatever works for you, and you can do it each year.

In order to start or add a tradition, try to figure out what you enjoyed the most as a family. Ask your kids what they remember from the last holiday and see if that could become part of your holiday each time. The most important requirement of any tradition is the ability for it to reconnect the generations with the fond memories that matter this year and every year.

Each time we share any family tradition we re-create a sense of family history and generate memories. As we do so, we become part of a seamless family link from the past to the present and we offer a gift to future generations.

In Our Memories: Charles "Shabazz" Rock

Many of my children's early memories involved their late brother Charles. It is fitting to remember him here because he was a huge part of our family. There are good and not-so-good memories with him, but the good outweighs the bad. It is important to dwell *more* on the positive and celebrate the life of the person who is no longer with us.

Ann: When Charles came to stay with the family, he was automatically accepted. There was no differentiation between him and the other children. I remember him as a loving person; everybody was OK with him.

My stepson, Charles, had a troubled life—including a stint in juvenile detention and prison—before he came to us in his late teens. He needed a good influence—who could be better than his own father? So, we welcomed him into our family. The kids took to him immediately. They fell in love with him.

It was a wonderful thing how quickly he fit in and fell into line. Even though he wasn't used to routines or even being on time for dinner, to see the positive changes in him was something, and a good example. He began to blossom into the outstanding person he would become.

Charles went on to earn a master's degree in business and worked for a prominent New York company. He was in the young executive program and was on the swim team for his company. He dated and later married his childhood sweetheart, Michelle Richardson (Randy's sister).

Although it seemed like he was a success in every measure of the word, the alcoholism that was always in his background took control of him, later in his life.

Alcoholism is a terrible disease that can tear a family apart. It is definitely a disease; it was hard for everyone to see him in the throes of it. Although he had love from everyone (he was Lola's favorite

Brian: It is hard to capture the full positive impact Charles made on all of our lives. One thing, he was a child of my father's youth, which meant he was old enough to be a second father to me. He was my younger, cooler, more athletic "father." He didn't have to be practical like my dad. One time he bought me a Hot Wheels after my father said I'd outgrow it too soon so he wouldn't buy it.

Randy Richardson: In some ways I think Charles was a role model for Chris and me—I think he influenced Chris's style. When I met him, he was a fine example of what you wanted a young black man to be. He had a great job, he was handsome in his Afro, and we were all impressed. Chris hung one of his big platform shoes from a pull string on the light as a decoration.

uncle), it wasn't enough to save him from himself. Ultimately, he died from pneumonia. All of us miss him.

Once again, when we tell the "Shabazz" stories, they sustain and inspire us. When I think of Charles, I think of the fun the boys used to have with him and all the memories they shared. He was such a handsome young man, and what a fashion plate (one of the boys used his crazy platform shoes as bookends in his room—can you imagine that?). I think what I most remember was his hunger and enthusiasm for reading and learning—he wanted to read everything and anything. His loving legacy, especially for the children when they were young, will never be lost as long as all of us remember him.

Shared memories of the sweet and the sad, the wonderful, the hilarious, and the "wish it could have been better" times are all part of the fabric of a family. The births and the passings and all that is in between make up the riches of a family's legacy: the treasure of remembrances. Create as many positive memories as you can—they will strengthen all the members of your family all of their lives.

Remember Mama Rock's Rules and Strategies

- Share "Before You Were Born" Memories

    Kids love to hear how much they were loved, even before they were born. Talk up those days, especially before a new baby arrives.

- Know Your Family by Your Traditions

  "We always" traditions are the foundation of strength and comfort for children and adults.

- Narrow the Generation Gap with Holiday Traditions

  Include all ages in your holiday activities to bring everyone closer.

- Follow the Pajama Principle

  The most meaningful traditions don't have to be stuffy, but they do have to provide a feeling of belonging.

- Good Memories Don't Have to Cost Good Money

  There is a wealth of good times that don't need big cash. Some of the simplest things can become the most memorable.

- Keep that "Junk"—It Could Be an Heirloom

  Be sure to save all kinds of family treasures—like your children's artwork, poems, awards, and memorabilia—not only expensive valuables.

- Talk Up Your Memories Through an Oral History

  Don't just remember the objects of the past—remember the stories of the living who remember the past.

- There's Always Something to Be Thankful For

  Every holiday or special occasion should celebrate the spirit of appreciation—not just Thanksgiving.

- **Keep Santa and the Tooth Fairy for as Long as You Can**

    As long as there are parents and children, all the magical traditions should exist without age limit—at least in our hearts.

- **It's Never Too Late for Traditions**

    Begin now to build a tradition bridge from the present to the future. It's the way to keep family connected and to re-create a rich legacy of remembrances.

{ 10 }

Spirituality Is Not
Just for Sundays

THOSE WHO DELVE INTO ANY spiritual life always come up
with the same core of truth—that it is all about connecting
with a higher power than us. I told my kids it did not matter
what their religion was, but it did matter that they believed in
something larger than themselves—that was the heart of it. When
you help your child develop a spiritual foundation, you give him a
guide to a moral and ethical life, a guide to treating people right,
and a deep, abiding sense of confidence that he will pass on to
his children.

People so often believe that spirituality has to be in the style of: I am always in church or whooping and hollering on my knees 24/7. That's not it at all. It is your personal walk with your God, your divine connection, that powerful feeling inside of you that changes the way you see everything. It can shape your entire life, which is what it is supposed to do. If you don't have that strong, sacred core on the inside, all the laying on of hands and all the ministers, priests, or rabbis in the world can't reach you to become a better person.

Spirituality Is Special Every Single Day

Spirituality should be an everyday part of everything you do. Just like church should not be a Sunday thing, spiritual beliefs need to be a part of your children's daily life. Your beliefs provide comfort when things go wrong, so what better gift could you give your children than to help them believe in something more than themselves? When everyone is gone, when all else fails, your child has something greater that can assure him (and you) that he will never be alone. That is the fail-safe. This is your promise that you have prepared your child for the world in the best way possible—whether you are with your child or not.

It's not easy to have our children turn out well. Spirituality is definitely an anchor in tough times, not only as you raise the kids, but later, when the kids have to go out into this crazy world. When my kids were growing up, I did a lot of praying and I still do. Prayer nourishes the person who prays. I don't care how you pray—on your knees, at church, in a car, at the beach—because it is the act of praying, of acknowledging a higher power, which helps lead to a more spiritual life. When you have a spiritual life, it will help you through all kinds of things—and when you teach it to your children, it is the bedrock of support for them all their lives.

In my day, growing up in the South the way I did, church was so important. I had a fear of God, the fear of "doing stuff" because he was *always watching*. I feared God more than I feared my parents, which is saying something. After all, one of the worst things to say to a child in my day was "wait until Daddy comes home" (in some homes that is still true). Seriously, I still feared God more because after my parents punished me, it was over. Who knew when God would get me for what I might do or even what I might think.

Today, things are different than when I grew up. For one thing, there is not much fear of God (it is not as popular to teach that viewpoint as it was when I was a child) or respect for authority (that's part of the reason) for that matter. Sadly, there's not as much talk about "wait till Daddy comes home," only because many kids don't have a father. That makes it even more important to help your children find a belief system to help them—not out of fear, but out of your desire for them to become fully developed people with a sense of honor and a respect for themselves and the world around them.

The Church Is Not a Convenience Store

Too many parents think the church or temple is the only place for their children to learn about their faith—it should all be up to the house of worship. You know, stop by on the Sabbath (especially on Sunday when other things are closed) and pick up just what you need from church or send the kids to Sunday school—that should do it.

In the same way we cannot expect the schools to teach our children everything, neither can we expect any church to do it all. Parents, you have the ability to teach your children the importance of faith by your example—not only in religious doctrine, but by what goes on in your home (for example, the love between parents, and their shared commitment to a home where values such as respect, helping others, forgiveness, patience, and loyalty are as important as anything they simply "hear" or "read" in church). After all, you are your child's first teachers. At the same time, what are you teaching your child if you get dressed up on a Sunday and go to church without your kids—or drop them off and go out to breakfast? What is that about? What does that say to your child? If you do go, attend as a family.

Music artist Bruce Carroll said it right in the lyrics of his song "I'd Rather See a Sermon Than Hear a Sermon":

> *Actions speak much louder than all the words can say*
> *That's why I'd rather see a sermon than hear one any day.*

When I was growing up, I went to Sunday school or services each week, rain or shine—my grandfathers were ministers, too. Until my brother got his bike, we walked at least a mile to get there. Later, I rode on his handlebars.

After I left home, I did not go as often. I didn't require my children to be in Sunday school every Sunday. Even though our church attendance was sporadic, my parents had planted the seeds of my beliefs about what was right. This included a basic "treat people the way you want to be treated" and a conviction that everything was subject to a higher power. This is what I tried to instill in my children by what we talked about and by my actions. Nothing could be more important.

Julius came from a minister's family where he had to go to church every Sunday when he was growing up. By the time I met him, he had developed different views. I would say he was spiritual in the deepest sense rather than religious in the "always in church," organized religion sense. Believe me, Julius was a sermon you could see. His father, Reverend Allen Rock, may have given some dramatic sermons, but Julius was a living sermon of good living, fine examples, and quiet spirituality. He helped cultivate that in all our children.

Prayer Gives You Power

Children need to know that you know how to pray, that you know the value of prayer, and that you are praying for their best outcome. Family prayer can become a way for kids to learn, if they can listen to prayers by their parents and other family members. They also can learn to share their feelings and ideas about God.

You can begin to teach your children to pray by saying regular prayers such as grace or specific bedtime prayers. It is comforting for them to have a nighttime prayer like "Now I lay me down to sleep . . ."—what a wonderful thing for a child to lie down and trust there is something bigger than Mommy or Daddy looking out for him. Even if something happened, he knows he will be OK. That's security.

For a young child, prayer can be translated into an expression of gratitude and it can become an everyday thing. Many families have a prayer gathering where they hold hands and pray before they go away from each other. In the old days, the elders would actually call to a child and bless him. Parents used to bless their kids to protect them. Most of us don't do those things anymore, but we probably should.

> { MAMA'S MOJO Don't wait to begin prayers until
> your kids are "old enough" or until they are in Sunday
> school or religious classes. Keep prayers short and sweet if
> the kids are young, otherwise they will lose interest. Keep
> the language of your prayers understandable to everyone.
> Listen, kids catch on fast—if Mom or Dad always sighs out
> loud when the other one says, "let us pray," what do
> you think a child will conclude? }

People are taught much too often to pray for miracles and for miraculous things to happen. Sometimes, that is the only time someone prays. I think it is a better idea to pray for simple things and to associate all of the blessings we have with God—not something miraculous. This is important: teach your kids that not all their prayers will be answered.

After all, God, like many fathers, sometimes says no. Besides, what if your kids really received some of the dumb things they asked for? I think they would get messed up. God knows the reasons for granting prayers or not; we don't see the big picture.

I believe in the power of prayer for life. It has kept me grounded. When I get up in the morning my first prayer is of thanksgiving—the gift of this day the Lord has made—and it continues throughout the day. It teaches us humility. I passed this on to my kids, and I think it is a wonderful thought to pass on to your children.

Help Your Child Search for Meaning

I know that some parents feel rejected or blame themselves if their children choose a different religion than the one shared by the family. I don't buy into that. Kids are searching for meaning—and they need to search until they find out what makes sense for them. Andi said that truth was the most important thing I ever shared about faith. She now attends a Catholic church, which is different from my upbringing. I'm just glad she's going to church so she can take time to hook up spiritually and take time out of her life each week to think about higher things.

When Brian became a minister, I was surprised. Then again, he told me that, because he was taught by example, he wanted to help other people find what he had found—a spiritual awakening and a way of living; he said he couldn't keep it to himself.

It Is Important to Honor Your Children

One way to guide your action in the gift of parenting is to honor a child. Why honor your child? Because your child is God's gift to you. God has said of a child: "I knew you before I placed you in your mother's womb."

When you honor your child, you help bring into being a confident, self-assured, independent, "I can take on the world" individual. Anyway, the best way to teach a child to honor others—parents, neighbors, loved ones—is to honor and respect *them*.

One way to honor a child is to take the time to be aware of his differences within your family. You honor a child's spirit and individuality when you take time to accept him and his quirks. You honor his gifts, creativity, and good qualities. You can even honor him as he tries to improve bad qualities like impatience—especially if you help him find ways to improve them.

Nothing should be so pressing that you can't take a few minutes for your child. Sometimes, that's all he needs from you—to see your warm, loving smile and a big hug the minute you walk in the door.

Another important way to honor your children is for you to spend time with each child individually. For example, normally, I wouldn't choose to watch what Jordan watches on TV. Listen, the program is only on for only thirty minutes. What does it really take to sit and watch something if he says he wants to share it with me?

From the children's earliest ages, I made a plan to spend private time with each child. It can be as simple as making time to do what a child likes to do. For example, my Brian loved to talk about everything in a current book he was reading—and I do mean everything. It honored him for me to listen to his thoughts about his book. All of these behaviors set an example for your kids to honor each other, too.

Chris and Andre sold Sunday papers to make spending money. Once, Chris came home from selling his assigned newspapers on Sunday morning. His brother Andre had to work late the evening before. So, Chris took Andre's share of the newspapers and sold them for him. Then he gave him every penny of the money. He honored his brother and experienced the joy of giving.

One of the times I saw how much respect Julius had for our children was when we went to shop for new bunk beds for the kids. At the store, a salesman came over and suggested a much lower-priced mattress than we had selected—he implied that kids were just kids and could sleep on anything, so why bother with a

Ally: Sometimes, Dad would come home (he worked at night) just as I was getting up. The master bedroom was on the parlor floor. I loved to run down the stairs from my upstairs bedroom and jump into his arms. Sometimes, he'd hear me coming and say, "Ally, I'm too tired to catch you today." I kept on coming anyway, and you know what? He always caught me and we'd laugh. Those few moments together meant the world to me.

Tony: I promised Kenny I would come to his kindergarten graduation, but that morning, I was lazy. My father said, "You promised your brother you would come to his graduation and you said no?" I went. After I saw Kenny's happy face, I understood the need to honor my promises. It taught me something big.

better-quality mattress. That upset Julius. He told the salesman, "No, you've got it wrong. I can sleep on anything. Parents need to provide the best we can for our children." We left the store and went down the street to another store. We found a new type of bedding called "bunkies"—which was top-of-the-line—and that's what we bought.

He also honored our children when he never allowed them to be displaced if we had more overnight company than our guest room could handle. He would rather we give up our bed and sleep in the den before we made the children give up their beds.

Chris and Malaak also honor their children in many ways. Because travel is so much a part of the entertainment business, they try to have the same routine and comforting items for the children when they are on the go. Chris bathes the kids every night, if at all possible, no matter where they are. Malaak makes things seem familiar by having another set of books and toys for their two homes (on both coasts) and other locations where they stay as a family.

> **MAMA'S MOJO** If you are in the armed services, on the road, or are just making a trip across country to visit relatives, get an extra one of your child's favorite book, game, or toy and bring it with you. If you travel between two places on a regular basis, leave one set in both places. You don't have to get extras for everything. Just a few will do the trick. By doing so, you honor a child's need for structure and continuity. This allows him to cope more easily—and don't forget your religious reading materials.

It's Also Important to Honor
Your Father and Mother

As we honor our children, so our children need to honor us. In many ways, the respect for authority that is learned at home is the key to a child's success. I don't think honoring a parent means fearing a parent. Instead, it implies regard and compliance with parents' word and the rules of the household, which the parents have created. It starts at the beginning as parents connect with their child from his first moments as a baby. Parents, set up that trust, and once you are trusted, you can set limits and establish the rules. You can create the right environment from which to develop your child's God-given abilities.

This is the only commandment of the Ten Commandments that comes with a promise from God: if you honor your parents, you will be blessed, and will see that your days are long on this earth. Perhaps this makes sense in another way, too, because parents can be a child's example of God on earth—if they do it right. That is as it should be. Parents are the closest things to God when they give selfless love and provide tenderness and forgiveness. That is the connection.

One thing fascinated my boys when they visited my parents during the summers—they still talk about it. They got a chance to see that, when I was in the presence of my father, he was still honored and respected by me. My father noticed that my kids slipped up when they visited him and didn't say their bedtime prayers every night. When I returned to get the kids, my father told me he was disappointed in them—right in front of the children. He said, "These are your children, but you are still my child and I want you to do something about it." The boys looked at me, then back at my father like they were watching a ping-pong match. They saw that I still valued his wisdom and respected his judgment—because I agreed with him. It was powerful for my kids to see this. Our children need to see us honoring our parents, too—as long as it is appropriate. It's never too late to start.

Don't Make Promises You Can't Keep— If You Can Help It

Breaking promises is detrimental to your family's integrity and to the development of a sense of spirituality in your home. Children need to know they can count on you, and that you will honor your word to them.

Sometimes that isn't easy. One day, I had promised Tony and Andre that I would take them out to lunch as a treat for doing so well—parents could take kids out of public schools for lunch on special occasions in those days. So, they waited outside the office for me to pick them up. On the way, I had a flat tire (that was before cell phones). Meanwhile, a teacher suggested they should go ahead and have lunch in the cafeteria because it seemed like I wasn't going to arrive. Andre relented and went to lunch. Tony sat, waited, and waited some more. Finally, when he could hear my heels clicking down the hall, he said to his teacher, "I knew my mom was going to come. She never breaks promises to us."

Understand this: your children begin to grasp the concept of faith when they learn to believe in you and your promises. They respect you when you say something and stand by it. You don't blow them off. When they can trust you if you say something will be done, you have set the stage for them to trust the promise of a spiritual faith.

> MAMA'S MOJO Single parents, don't let your children feel the pain of rejection if you cancel visits without good reason or break a promise to them. Be realistic about what you can do. It is critical to keep your promises and set the stage for your children to believe.

Get Prepared with "On-the-Job" Spiritual Training

We had a strong belief system in our home; we believed in God—he was the head of our house. Among the ways we chose to express that belief was by example. Spirituality is like integrity in parenting—you must live it and display it to your kids. It is a personal one-on-one discovery for them. Yes, it is a little like "on-the-job training." For instance, if I get too much change at the grocery store, I return it (and make sure my kids see me do it). That illustrates honesty and integrity.

If I find out someone is laid up, or a man is out of work, I can do something to help without expecting something back. It's easy to go

Brian: Church and religion were never anything that was forced on us. People always say children learn by example. My parents showed the way; it was almost like "on-the-job training" in spirituality. As kids, we couldn't fully comprehend a lot of concepts; instead we learned through seeing it and living it.

to the phone or electric company, for instance, and put something down toward his bill (let the utilities say "anonymous" paid it so he won't think there was a mistake). There are so many ways to help people without embarrassing those you are helping or calling attention to yourself. Let your kids understand this, or better yet, bring them along with you on these special "errands."

Although Chris and Malaak read the Bible each evening to their girls, they also show them by word and example that they believe in a higher power. This consistency comforts and strengthens the children. Whether you read the Bible or not, the integrity with which you live is important for your children to experience.

What My Kids Learned About Good Deeds on Halloween

My older boys had a "living example" of the power of good deeds during one Halloween in Brooklyn. An elderly, disagreeable woman lived next door to us. She was so mean she would snatch a child's toy away if it fell in her yard. Anyway, on Halloween some kids from another street pelted some of the brownstone houses on our street with eggs. No one hit ours, but plenty hit the cranky lady's house next door. Those eggs stuck to the bricks and made a big mess. I gave the boys a bowl of soapy water and told them to go out and clean her house. The boys protested something fierce. "She's so mean and nasty," they cried. I told them they had to do it. She peeked out the windows and said nothing. After they were done, she came out and thanked the boys. She told them she was wrong about them—and she added, "When I'm wrong, I admit I was wrong. I am sorry."

Brian: I was blown away when the mean old lady from next door came out and was nice to us after we had helped her. It impressed me how good deeds can make big changes in people. I still believe that. My mother gave us a big lesson about being good to neighbors (literally), no matter what. She didn't just say it, she showed us how.

Celebrating Nature Is Like Saying a Prayer

If you look for it, you will find a higher power in all of nature, even the simplest things. Teach your children the wonders of nature and how to be aware of what is around them. I call Jordan my "moon child"—ever since he was a tiny child, I would take him outside to look at the moon. He is almost seventeen now, but he will still call me outside to look at a particularly beautiful moon and find wonder in it.

When you honor the lives of the greatest or smallest creatures, you are honoring the environment and everything God made for you. Take a minute with your child and stop your car rather than run over a turtle in the road. Put him on the other side, safely.

Celebrate nature with your child. Simply look up at the clouds and try to identify shapes and creatures. Jump in a pile of leaves and smell the air. Or, go out after a snowstorm and make snow "angels" in fresh snow; lie on your backs and move your arms—while touching the snow—toward your head and toward your feet in an arch. Get up and look at your "angels"—you'll see the wings. All these things get your child in touch with nature and a sense of the bigger world.

Don't forget—it is you, the parent, who plants the seeds of spiritual values in your children, not only by what you teach them about your God, but by the way in which you live your life. Treat each other with love, respect, and forgiveness—help your children understand the importance of this. When all else fails, your child's spiritual background will sustain him.

Share the power of prayer and respect for all of God's creations. When you do this, it will complete your best job as a parent and give your child a strong foundation and an important legacy.

Remember Mama Rock's Rules and Strategies

■ **Spirituality Is Not Just for Sundays**
  Help your child develop a strong spiritual foundation—it will give him confidence and the assurance that he will never be alone.

■ **The Church Is Not a Convenience Store**
  No house of worship can teach everything—parents need to teach their kids values and the belief in something larger than themselves.

- Honor Your Children

    The best way to teach children to honor and respect others is to honor and respect them.

- Honor Your Parents

    In many ways, the respect for authority that is learned at home is the key to a child's success.

- Don't Make Promises You Can't Keep—If You Can Help It

    Children learn the concept of faith when they can trust you and believe in your promises.

- Try "On-the-Job" Spiritual Training

    Show your children, by example, how you live your faith by how you treat others and how you act with honor and caring. It's "on-the-job" training for spiritual development.

- Celebrating Nature Is Like Saying a Prayer

    There is a higher power in all of nature; show your children how to be aware of it.

Acknowledgments

TO GOD BE THE GLORY. Thanks first to God, Who makes it all possible.

I am grateful to the following people who have been a part of the creation of this book: Melissa Flashman and Trident Media Group, and Kathryn Huck and the HarperCollins publishing family for embracing this project; Heather Jackson for being the first to think I could do a parenting book; Dr. Barbara Mackoff for her support and encouragement; Terrie Williams for her enthusiastic encouragement; Johanna D. Wilson, of *The Sun News*,

Myrtle Beach, who first put the "rules" on the map, and to Reverend Lorenzo Smalls for being there for me.

Jeanette Ard's hospitality at her Humidor Bistro in Georgetown provided the ultimate working environment for us to create, and the kind staff at California Dreaming in Surfside Beach allowed us to work endless hours while providing endless cups of coffee.

Thank you to "Wally B" for being my Regis for nine years on *The Mom Show*, and to the Reverend Al Sharpton for standing tall with me.

Thank you to Virgil and Sage Graham for sharing Valerie with me. And to Valerie Graham for taking my words and stories and putting them all together into this special book. Please know this could not have happened without you and all your hard work and dedication. My thanks, love, and gratitude for a job well done.

To Julius, thank you for the wonderful family you and I have created. To my children and all of my family for the stories and memories—may they continue each time we gather together.

—Rose Rock